IS THIS FOREVER, OR WHAT?

Poems & Paintings from Texas

The Dancer
RONALD KOLODZIE

IS THIS FOREVER, OR WHAT?

Poems & Paintings from Texas

SELECTED BY

Naomi Shihab Nye

GREENWILLOW BOOKS

An Imprint of HarperCollins*Publishers*

IN MEMORY

Vassar Miller, Joe Stanco
A. C. Greene, Joanie Whitebird
Albert Huffstickler

AND

James Marion White Bear Cody

"What I choose to pursue
is the gleam in my eye
the dream on the fly
a story to spin.

But I can only write out of where I've been."
—SUSAN FORD WILTSHIRE

LIBRARY OF CONGRESS CATALOGING-IN-PUBLICATION DATA
Is this forever, or what? : poems & paintings from Texas / selected by Naomi Shihab Nye.
p. cm.
"Greenwillow Books."
Summary: A collection of poetry and full-color artwork from Texas.
ISBN 0-06-051178-8 (trade). ISBN 0-06-051179-6 (lib. bdg.)
1. Children's poetry, American—Texas. 2. Texas—Juvenile poetry. 3. Texas—In art—Juvenile literature.
[1. Texas—Poetry. 2. Texas—In art. 3. American poetry—Collections.] I. Nye, Naomi Shihab.
PS558.T418 2003 811.008'09282'09764—dc21 2003004441
First Edition
10 9 8 7 6 5 4 3 2 1

 Greenwillow Books

San Antonio

Tonight I lingered over your name,
the delicate assembly of vowels
a voice inside my head.
You were sleeping when I arrived.
I stood by your bed
and watched the sheets rise gently.
I knew what slant of light
would make you turn over.
It was then I felt
the highways slide out of my hands.
I remembered the old men
in the west side cafe,
dealing dominoes like magical charms.
It was then I knew,
like a woman looking backward,
I could not leave you,
or find anyone I loved more.

Naomi Shihab Nye

Untitled
ALBERTO MIJANGOS

INTRODUCTION

"We drove across Texas," people in other parts of the United States often say, "ONCE."

Although the title of this book springs from a poem about young romance by Carrie Fountain, it echoes a question asked by many travelers crossing Texas for the first time. "What do you mean, more than 700 miles from Beaumont to El Paso? Are you serious?"

Truly, it is farther from Texarkana in the east of the state to El Paso in the far west than from Chicago to New York. From the Oklahoma border at the north to Brownsville at the south, it's 903 miles. Whether you're driving Corpus Christi to Lubbock, McAllen to Wichita Falls, Dallas to Kingsville, Austin to Marfa, or Longview to Junction, you'd better fill your gas tank and pack water, apples, and corn chips.

Alaskans have a joke: they're talking about dividing their state in half, so Texas will be the THIRD largest state. This seems funny to me, though it took me a minute to understand it.

See, it is not true that Texans have no humility.

Those of us who live here for many years and savor long drives learn a few shortcuts and back roads. The length of the roads seems *normal*. A travel writer once made it his project to drive every single highway in Texas, including the lonesome farm roads and skinniest old pavements, writing about his huge journey for *Texas Monthly* magazine. For *years* I thought about him everywhere I drove. For all I know he's still out there, looking for the next turn.

Texas wanderers learn where the thickest bluebonnets coat the fields in radiant splendor every spring. We know where the cranes gather, where the best old cafes are tucked away, and which bakery sells cheese pockets (Haby's, in Castroville). We know the bird preserves sparkling with green jays along the Rio Grande, the incredible museums, the Tex-Mexican specialties, the eccentric small towns, the tortilla factories, Big Bend National Park, the bustling cities, quiet fields, strong individualists, fluent sky, the charismatic islands of Galveston and Padre . . . our precious treasures feel endless. But for Texans, wherever we live, it is the sense of generous horizon and spaciousness that surrounds and permeates our consciousness. Cities and towns have wide margins around them—we like that.

It's a big page on which to write or paint.

Texans are famously friendly. It's rumored that some states won't grant full-fledged status-of-belonging to residents even if they have lived in those states a very long time (you have to be *born there*). Texas is happy to claim you after ten minutes.

"We don't like Texas," two women said to me at a summer writing camp in an undisclosed U.S. location.

"Oh, no? Have you ever been there?"

"No," they said. "But we know we don't like it."

"How so?"

They looked at each other and shrugged, suddenly tongue-tied.

"Have you known some bad Texans or something?"

One blurted, "No! We've only known two Texans! Come to think of it, we LOVED both of them."

Here's a story. Texans favor stories. We tell them to ourselves as we drive.

As a college student at Trinity University in San Antonio, I joined a delegation traveling west to see the ancient caves filled with Native American pictographs out beyond Del Rio, near Comstock. A large reservoir was soon to be built in the region, and art historians worried that the increase in humidity in the atmosphere would cause the vivid wall paintings to deteriorate at a much more rapid rate than had happened over the previous years. (This has proven, alas, to be true.)

We took camping gear and ice chests. We hiked and stumbled in the rocky terrain. Our faces got sunburned. We loved the pictographs. We kept journals about the trip, drawing little pictographs on the pages. We cooked beans over an open fire. We sang.

In those days the bear population of west Texas was still diminished, so no one thought much about coming across a bear, though we probably would have been very happy to meet one. (The bear and mountain lion populations have increased dramatically since then in the wide Big Bend area. This seems a pleasant and mysterious antidote to the losses of modernity.) Someone caught a glimpse of a pack of wild pigs— javelinas—running off in the distance. A cloud of dust rose up from their hooves. Someone on our trip had once eaten one. Were they friendly?

They could be, someone said.

No, they are not, said someone else. They have sharp teeth. They wouldn't think twice about butting you over.

That night, sleeping on an open-air cot at some distance from the others,

Skylight
SCOTTIE PARSONS

under a spectacularly clear canopy of stars, I awakened to feel a heavy lump curled tightly against my stomach, nestled in my down sleeping bag. For a moment I thought I was at home and my cat was on my bed. Then I blinked and realized it was not a cat.

Sharp teeth, I recalled.

It was a baby javelina, snoring its piggy little snore, happily launched to dreamland.

Should I wake it up?

Not on your life. I petted the coarse hairs on its cozy back. I sang it a secret lullaby. When I finally fell asleep again, my dreams starred a small creature who knew more about grasses and trails and markings on walls than anyone with a driver's license knows. In the morning the baby javelina was gone, a pressed-in cavity in my sleeping bag still visible, but no one would believe me.

Poets are always making things up, said my friends.

Texas is a deep breath. I feel so relieved every time my plane lands in Texas again and I see that characteristic dusky live-oak green, unlike any other green I know. A college friend from New Jersey used to say, when people asked why he had come to Texas for four years, "I figure the rest of my life is going to be hard. I'm stocking up on warm breezes to be ready for it."

Texans like little things as much as big ones. How else could a miniature town called Little Dime Box have persisted so long? Or a town called Welfare that is simply an abandoned general store and a gracious series of fields? Arrowheads, limestone "friendship" rocks with perfect holes in them, tiny fluted shells on Mustang Island. Towns advertise themselves as the "friendliest little town" or the "biggest little town" and feel proud.

We do *not* boast. We're just enthusiastic.

The most surprising question about Texas I've ever been asked is how we can stand to live without any trees.

Except for some treeless stretches (okay—maybe hundreds of miles in all directions) in the panhandle, Texas is a tree-lover's paradise. From the dense deep green piney woods of east Texas to the swampy bayou oaks around Houston, to the native pecan groves and semi-tropical abundance of San Antonio and the live oaks and mesquites of Central Texas and the hill country and the pollen-rich cedars that half our population are allergic to, to the proud palms of the coastal regions and the Rio Grande Valley, we have all the trees we need.

We have droughts and floods. Days when the temperature drops 30 degrees in a few hours. Northers, when the cold winds roar down upon us . . . hailstorms, tornadoes, and hurricanes. Dust storms, sometimes. But mostly we have many, many days of deep sunshine and quintessential blue sky.

Yes, it gets hot here. But the hottest I have been in the last few years was in Toronto and upstate New York. Check us out in January for balance.

To anyone from elsewhere who still thinks we're bereft, hey, what's it like living without a wide margin, huh?

The poets and painters in this anthology represent the beautiful diversity, the multiplicity, of our state—they are wonderful artists doing great work, all of them, even the ones currently sojourning elsewhere. I feel bad, being a friendly Texan myself now, about all the people we *aren't* including, which is (once again) due to that old issue of space. Trust that there are many more terrific poets and painters in and from Texas, not only because the state is so large but because it is so energetically creative. May you enjoy this rich sampling.

By the way, at least half of the people in this book probably own no boots or cowboy hats. Most may never have ridden a horse seriously—as in, to get anywhere—except maybe Leslie Ullman and Paulette Jiles. I think Paulette took a cell phone. Ann Alejandro favors a mule.

NAOMI SHIHAB NYE
San Antonio, Texas
2003

San Antonio Fatso Watso Table
ROLANDO BRISEÑO

The Orchard

I went to the orchard where no one for years has planted or pruned,
Where wild-suckering limbs break under the weight of the crowding fruit,
   and hackberries grow choking the younger trees;
Where the gaps mature trees filled are the gaps between a poor woman's teeth,
   and the ground turned by the harrow when moisture was a thing remembered
   is the cracked lip of a neglected child,
And the yellow weeds waist high the hair the dead keep growing.

And though from a distance the leaves dull-green suggested the voices of those
   who summers gathered each fruit in its turn—
   the tart plums, the warm peaches, the ruddy pears (remarking
   how unusually sweet this year the grapes sprawling over the fence)—
Up close they crackled, a brush fire spreading from where for days
   it smoldered under the scorched grass.

I went to the one tree which bears every year without fail its pears, the birds
   flapping their hollow bones at my approach.
Through the leaves a small bat uncurled like a wisp of smoke.
And for every pear I gathered there was one too ripe, and one the birds had pecked,
   and one full of black weevils, and a dozen the masked raccoon
   knocked to the ground,
Fruit once firm and good, given to the boot's press,
And hornets rising each above a rotten globe.

Robert A. Ayres

Climbing the Caprock

Wrinkled caliche gulches give way at last
to the long plateau, like breath, a place
of restfulness. Here you can close
your eyes and pretend you don't exist
except in this moment the canyons and plains
dream tonight of something under moonlight.

Once, after driving hours, we stopped;
my brother parked beside the road and slept—
long prairies, the clear restful sky,
and somewhere water crackling all night long,
splattering against a pavement or stone.
Was it a river? A water fountain running

all night? Or just a spring leaping into air
from stone veins deep within the hills?
Next morning we drove on; since then,
my brother's gone, and a million miles passed.
But some nights the water comes back. Crackling
in my mind, it gleams in moonlight, bright
again a moment before it turns back underground.

Roger Jones

Texas in the Afternoon

Barley grass in winter, rude-boy lush
sweet pea seeds in my palm like grains

of yeast, and the same promise of ardor

The neighbors' cat lying on the carport floor
flees, always jumping over the same spot in
   the fence

I love her ritualized terror, her American
   sense of drill
She sprawls behind the kitchen minutes
   later, asleep

Midmorning grackles caw, the silver-blue
mint on their wings, a theft from the sun

The live oak shading three front yards
The squirrels store, lose and retrieve

Exile
your ninety-nine names
trill the tip of my tongue

Time now to sing what I've wrought
into blessing—indigenous, though scant

Khaled Mattawa

Shelter (Jane's house)
JAN TIPS

Praise to That Which

Does not need us to praise it
To the oceans—deep—before—and after us
To mountains (despite quarries)
To rivers (despite dams)
To waterfalls and national forests
To the very air (threatened by us)
To the earth and its strong song
(May we learn her words—and sing along)
and praise what we do not yet understand
allow it to live within our little fenced lands.

Thom the World Poet

Resting Hummer
MELANIE FAIN

"THEIR LIFE, THEIR JOY"

The Line of Days

Looking to the Sun
ISABETH BAKKE HARDY

Four Generations

Before it burned, he heard her sing at the opera house
and threw two yellow roses. They slid
between floor and hem, touched
her slipper's instep.

She watched him walk at the USO dance,
a strange splay in his hips, and thought
I had better get used to that.

At the rally, he takes her hand. She thinks of how, later, sitting
on the bed, she will tell her sister.

One hand to your face, I am astonished: this is the softness of a pear
    at breakfast.

Moira Muldoon

EL ICE-CREENERO / The Ice-Cream Man

(FOR SHORTY)

What you got today, Shorty?

I got your
Bullets
Popsicles
Push-ups
Fudgsicles

We knew when he was coming down
the neighborhood
the tiny tinkling jingle
   of his ice-cream cart
signaled he's *Here*

suddenly,
baseball games stopped
footballs fell
phones dropped
screen doors blew out
&
kids would crowd in wonder at
his three-wheel bike

the little row of bells running
along the length of the handlebars
his skin bronzed by a Texas-oven sun
wiping his face with a white handkerchief
cabby hat pushed back on his head
smiling as he opened the lid of his icy
   treasure
chest on wheels letting us treat our sweaty
   faces
to the blast of ice cold air before making
   our final deals

Tenk you boys

&
he would ride away
small cracked shoes pedaling
down the baked streets
of the melting day

Fernando Esteban Flores

Body Shop

Starlings,
erupting into openness,
flit from trees like metal shavings
off the '72 Cadillac
at Arturo's Paint and Body Shop.
The southside is echoing
the grace of sunset
as a cumbia plays loudly in the shop,
leaking its brown rhythm
onto Arturo's arms,
mixing with flecks of rust and paint
as he corrects mistakes made by others.
He bends into his work,
sweating droplets that bead on the
    dusty floor,
the shop humid
with his dedication to craft.
This trade, this way of life,
working the violence from warped
    machines,
has been his best school.
He has learned about people
and business,
learned how preciseness can be stretched
for hours and hours,
investing himself into making things
    once bent
straight again.
Arturo envisions the '72 Cadillac perfect
and painted yellow.
Inside his shop, he doesn't see
the narrowing day, the way light stretches
across the Nova out front
he finished just yesterday.
He doesn't see that,
in the leaning sunlight, the hood
of the Nova, like a bird's wing, just
shimmers and shimmers.

Ben Tremillo

And Every Town Its Dairy Queen

In Texas, every podunk town
has a Dairy Queen,
where old men in Stetsons
or John Deere caps
gather between naps,
burgers fat as bibles
dripping grease in their laps.
They stare at a landscape lit
like an overexposed photo.
Sunlight glints off windshields
till every eye turns inward
to the kinder light of memory.
Their lives tick like combines cooling;
their stories, old ropers worn thin.

But it's comforting here,
where the waitress has hair as big
as her heart, and flirts
as she refills their coffee.
Finally, the black cups cool
and the old men hoist their bellies up
from the booths, crank their frames
out to the parking lot.
And one hand waving
and one foot in the car,
they pause to watch a strange wind brew
as a dust devil scampers up from a field,
grabs their hats, and runs.

Beverly Caldwell

To the Desert

I came to you one rainless August night.
You taught me how to live without the rain.
You are thirst and thirst is all I know.
You are sand, wind, sun, and burning sky,
The hottest blue. You blow a breeze and brand
Your breath into my mouth. You reach—then *bend*
Your force, to break, blow, burn, and make me new.
You wrap your name tight around my ribs
And keep me warm. I was born for you.
Above, below, by you, by you surrounded.
I wake to you at dawn. Never break your
Knot. Reach, rise, blow, *Sálvame, mi dios,*
Trágame, mi tierra. Salva, traga, Break me,
I am bread. I will be the water for your thirst.

Benjamin Alire Sáenz

Blue Sticks Flying Connected

At Grandma's I made a mason jar a light
and from the river marsh
caught a bucket of new frogs,
putting more on top, more on top.

Sunday morning, in pink dress,
I saw the sag of hide between
the bodies and the legs. Daddy said
it was too late; I couldn't take them back.

Sandra Gail Teichmann

Shelling Pecans

The crack crack of shells
called to his neighbors like a lure.
My grandfather, sitting in his white-enameled RCA rocker,
stooped over the grocery bag of shells between his knees,
my grandmother's mixing bowl, half filled with meats, beside him.
Two nuts disappeared into his hand, pressed shell against shell.
The sudden release as one shell failed sent a sharp call
into the warm fall air. Soon
two or three gathered on the porch,
shell-filled bags between their knees,
amidst a chorus of snaps,
comparing the cost of crops
and eating the broken meats.

Years later, my father and I sit
side by side, two levered nutcrackers
gripping our kitchen table.
We fall into rhythm, a competition
to reach the last nut,
the sprung clap of the nutcrackers
and the shoosh of broken shells
into the paper bags between our knees
our only conversation.

Marissa C. Martínez

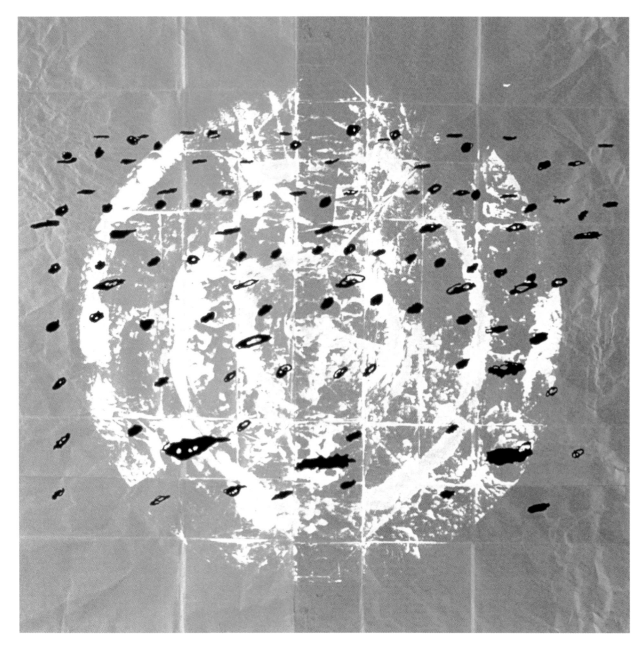

Note
ANNETTE LAWRENCE

"Drive Friendly"

(TEXAS INTERSTATE ROAD SIGN)

How to accomplish this latest admonition
from the Texas Department of Public Safety?
Will I become a better driver if I take one
or both hands off the wheel and wave gaily
at approaching automobiles? Or blink my lights?

Or toot the horn in amicable fashion
when passing through sleeping neighborhoods?
To operate a motor vehicle deep in this part
of Texas, do I need a ten-gallon hat
to tip to every woman driver?

I don't observe my fellow Texans driving
especially friendly, especially that S.O.B.
in the black Porsche convertible,
cutting me off in the middle lane.
Or the pickup who took away my right-of-way.

The Jeep behind me never dims its high beams.
The recreational vehicle up ahead zigs
and zags between lanes like a water beetle.
What gives them the license to drive
so unfriendly? Can't they read?

Native Texans know "Drive Friendly"
is merely the flip side of a warning:
In inclement weather it reads,
"Watch for Ice on Bridge"—
a sign giving Friendly the cold shoulder.

I envision a day when everyone will
Drive Friendly. Drivers will fling flowers
from open windows, blossoms sailing
from car to car in convivial exchange.
Highways will be strewn like Palm Sunday.

Or perhaps they fling confetti,
toilet paper fluttering down gaily—
even a trip to the Stop'n'Shop
will become a ticker tape parade,
every citizen a returning astronaut.

Balloons will hang like rubber clouds
over the beltways. Banners will festoon
traffic signals. Every driver will blow
kisses from car to car like Miss America,
and it will be friendly, friendly, friendly.

Robert Phillips

The Stove

JAMES COBB

Land of the Discount Price, Home of the Brand Name

My large magnetic car flag proudly displays Old Glory
as I drive to Family Dollar for the makings of a Fourth of July picnic.

I pledge allegiance to my MasterCard
that is honored in more stores than American Express.

Oh beautiful, those spacious aisles stacked high with seasonal items!

My country, 'tis of thee, sweet land of Lipton instant ice tea!

I've clipped a terrific recipe from Sunday's paper. A Betsy Ross
rectangular cake covered with strawberries, blueberries, and Cool Whip,
with a coupon for the Cool Whip.

On Independence Day, our all-American front porch shows our true colors
with patriotic bunting and bows, only $3.99 a yard (reg. $4.99).

Our backyard guests relax at our holiday picnic table,
thematically decorated with 10 oz. Stars and Stripes plastic tumblers,
matching table runner, paper plates and napkins from Dixie.

As my hubby grills the red meat and toasts the white buns under a blue sky,
our son shows the neighbor kids his World Peacekeepers Patriot Soldier,
a twelve-inch fully posable action figure that plays the national anthem.

Harryette Mullen

A Voice

Even the lights on the stage unrelenting
as the desert sun couldn't hide the other
students, their eyes also unrelenting,
students who spoke English every night

as they ate their meat, potatoes, gravy.
Not you. In your house that smelled like
rose powder, you spoke Spanish formal
as your father, the judge without a courtroom

in the country he floated to in the dark
on a flatbed truck. He walked slow
as a hot river down the narrow hall
of your house. You never dared to race past him,

to say, "Please move," in the language
you learned effortlessly, as you learned to run,
the language forbidden at home, though your mother
said you learned it to fight with the neighbors.

You liked winning with words. You liked
writing speeches about patriotism and democracy.
You liked all the faces looking at you, all those eyes.
"How did I do it?" you ask me now. "How did I do it

when my parents didn't understand?"
The family story says your voice is the voice
of an aunt in Mexico, spunky as a peacock.
Family stories sing of what lives in the blood.

You told me only once about the time you went
to the state capitol, your family proud as if
you'd been named governor. But when you looked
around, the only Mexican in the auditorium,

you wanted to hide from those strange faces.
Their eyes were pinpricks, and you faked
hoarseness. You, who are never at a loss
for words, felt your breath stick in your throat

like an ice-cube. "I can't," you whispered.
"I can't." Yet you did. Not that day but years later.
You taught the four of us to speak up.
This is America, Mom. The undo-able is done

in the next generation. Your breath moves
through the family like the wind
moves through the trees.

Pat Mora

At the Surplus Supply

a shadow cast
by a lone pecan
makes welcome shade
in this August heat

when a slight
breeze helps to bear
the waiting here
where the used furniture

has found its way
out of date
cracked & chipped
a broken leg

cyclopian computers
blinded as if by an
Odyssean stake
all have landed in

Beyond the Pale
JULIE SPEED

this warehouse of
the institutional discard
though at times
an item will be

recycled & upon a
day like this
one in need
of table or chair

in the midst of slabs
rusting metal in orange &
red gradations beside the
drought-bleached grass

comes to look them over
those have been replaced
to view them once it opens
waiting beneath this single tree

now stunted & stiff
the research labs nearby
for structural engineering
or archeological digs as

its rough bark coated with
a curry-colored lichen
limestone at its roots
standing here outside

it drops Algonquian fruit
for those will hunt & shell
for baking pies & pralines
a taste forever satisfies

whose cool relief from
a blinding summer sun
can never get enough of
will never go out of style

Dave Oliphant

Tiny Clay Doll with No Arms

Given to me by my sister as a gift,
the tiny Indian doll stands with no arms.

Given to me so I can raise my hands
and stop the world from getting closer.

Something has been taken from here—
a day when reaching out was death.

Something lost
with my own hands.

The doll stands three inches tall,
its brown head wrapped in a red scarf.

No arms, as if I could look at a body
and not welcome it back.

As if I knew what happened
to my grip on those things.

The clay doll stands on my bookshelf.
It stares out the window.

It does not have any arms.
I don't know why it was carved that way,

don't know what it means,
why the invisible palms hold everything.

When I touch it with a fingertip,
it leans against a book.

It does not fall.
When I set it back

on its bare feet,
I carefully use both hands.

Ray Gonzalez

Avocado Avenue

No, I don't live on Avocado Avenue,
and I've never been in the vicinity of avocado trees,
but I must confess
de vez en cuando I would rather be un vagabundo
hawking velvet avocados por los barrios de Aztlantejas USA.

Yes, I must confess: I am an avocado aficionado.
I will vouch for any avocado.
You see, avocados are not vociferous;
they are content to be versant with philosophical windowsills.
Who would vilify an avocado?
Visualize two avocados, two summer syllables on a windowsill,
ripening under Tonatiuh's vocabulario,
and you visualize world peace: paz, paz, paz.

Avocados are not equivocados;
they are not into hate, do not equivocate.
Aguacates are not into voodoo economics;
they just want a place on your Mexican plate.
But what must aguacates think?
Mexican food is chic; it's made the New York celebrity list.
It's Gucci bags next to guacamole bowls.

Meanwhile there are no revolutions on Guadalupe Street,
Only the blooming rosebushes by Rudy's Transmission.

Jacinto Jesús Cardona

*Tonatiuh—*Aztec god of the sun*

A Portrait of J. L. M.

We called him spirit of the place,
But he's more like a good old tree root.
Went off, a year gone, back to Rockport.
It seems, when he'd gone, us not even
Knowing it, everything fell apart.

       Wish I remembered
What he told me. This bit of town I
   landed in,
These railroad tracks he'd known, secret
Signs chalked on the freight wagon doors,
Hobos bivouacking, and how he'd drift
   across,
Talk with them. That was far back
In the Thirties, near enough to the yard
   on Seventh
He got our big old bamboo from,
   planted it.

       Wanderings, the split rail
Fences he built, him wiry then as now,
   bird-faced,
Out west of Sanantone; any job he
   could find

He put both hands to. He belonged with
Boilers of big ships, blue clouds
Of working people on the move,
   tumbleweed;
You do the most you can.

       Far out hereabouts
He'd gone courting, before big money
Rolled the roads in. Remember now,
Hummed the tune once, he did. They
   walked out
Through live oaks together, rocks, and
   cedar,
Listening to the trickle of the creek in
   Spring.
He sat his Mildred down, kissed her,
Same old tune in their heads.

       I ate her cakes
She'd later bring at Christmas down the
   hill,
Stopping to chat awhile, propped against
The doorpost, she'd laugh like anything
But sometimes she took ill.

Drain, spigots, carburetors,
The pump, I saw his knuckles whiten
When he flexed them, and later his hand
Shook, breath caught, and as he worked
His mouth helped, with twists and
   lippings.

       Rolled his own cigarettes;
   told me—
Here's this old songbook, found it at
   the county dump,
You want it? 1865—Irish songs. Irish
As his Indian scout grandfather had
   been. He'd
Told him of hilltops hereabouts

       Where the Indians hunkered,
Yawning. And how a coach might rumble
   by,
Gold or guns in it, stuff they could
   use. And how
Into this cave his grandfather went once,
   deep,
Now they've blocked it, but it goes
   underground
All the way from the lake to Tarrytown.
A volcano, too, he said.

       I might not believe it,
Not so far off, east, he found obsidian there,
Beyond where the highrise banks and
   turnpikes
And the military airport are. Trees,
He loved trees and drove miles to see them
At their best, the right time of the year.
Buckeye and catalpa in their first flower,
Chinaberry, dogwood.

       All birds had ordinary names,
Like redbird, but once in a while he'd speak
Old words, not from books but from
   Tennessee,
Like once he said "quietus." Always
Flesh in his words, and bone, and in his doings,
Not absent even from the way he'd knock
A bourbon back, straight, that was the way
He liked it, then roll another cigarette.

       For Mildred when her teeth
Fell out he whittled deer horn so she'd have
A biting edge up front. When he came by,
   dressed
Smart for a visit, he'd be wearing false
Rat teeth up front and give a wicked grin.
There was this park he kept,

He knew all the weeds in it,
All, and told how some weed sent
Cows mad and was taken too much liberty
   with
By them young folks as went out there
For a high time.

     Well, then he'd push off
In his battered pickup, headed for a
   honkytonk
Some place down the line. Why don't folks
   look at
That kind of man? Some say insight
Comes when you tell the individual
Get lost. What's all their deep droning talk
To him? He's too smart to think up
Revolutions, what's it, that perspective stuff?
Maybe he's nobody

     But he made things work,
Never slaving, nor ginrollizing. Made things
Shift and level with every breath he drew.
Had no grievance, spoke no ill of anyone
Or anything save spindly offshoots
Of tree roots that split drainpipes in the
   country,
Having ballooned in them, like brains
Got swole, so he'd say, with all the excrement.

Christopher Middleton

Yellow Head

LARRY GRAEBER

Cold Sauce

Every morning, every night,
I take the can of cat food from the fridge,
pry off the red plastic lid and peer
into the amber slime surrounding the mush.
Fumes of fish parts and meal rise
to mingle with the urgent cries.
I pour dry pellets into two bowls,
then divide the wet food—two plops—
and cover each round hard bit
with fragrant meaty sauce.
They hate the dry food alone,
but this concoction they devour,
crunching through the bad hard kernels,
licking at the cold sauce, and even its
   memory.
I stir and think, and stir and think,
"This is their life, their joy."
I can almost hear myself meowing.

Carol M. Siskovic

something

I look to you
keyboard
to say something to me
to bring me some intuitive wisdom
to console me, construct me,
converge me
to send me a message through
  my fingers
and your page
to reveal something
I wish I already knew.

I look to you
mailbox
to bring me something wonderful
to bring me something special
to change my life
to put something priceless
in my hands
that perhaps is already there
but I have no way of seeing.

I look to you
telephone
to transmit some important message
  to my ear
to give me news
good news
to make a connection
between me right here right now
and me someplace
in what I can be
and might become yet
but am still a stranger to.

I look to you
new day
perhaps tomorrow
perhaps tomorrow
always waiting for something
something
to happen.

Carmen Tafolla

Sandstorm
JOHN CATES

Ah Words

Ah words
we have old words
create whole languages
invent the word
new—

How deep
must words go
before emerging
once again in
silence?

How high
must words be
to make the word
music?

Robert Bonazzi

Connecting

A friend writes me—
a letter, can you believe—
tells me he'll look up my poem's subject
on the Internet, that endlessly ramifying root
holding us all together as we sway above
    the earth.

I think fine, I think
of the undulating flights of sandhill cranes
finding their way through a breezy heaven,
the rank perfumes of lakes and rivers below
    their guiding compass.

I think sure, I think
of the busy ants outside my door as they
    signal
one another to carry in more food,
the soft sibilance of antly scraping telling
    us the wisdom of saving.

I think yes, yes, why not
go to the cold glass page impersonal as
    a glove
go to it, the book is there these days,
or a view of it, though somewhere
in a dim library you'll find
        its original dusty and ignored
          its pages yellowing beneath
the smudged lipstick left there once by a girl
who read it in bed, her warm flesh pressing.

Robert Burlingame

David Talamántez on the Last Day of Second Grade

SAN ANTONIO, TEXAS, 1988

David Talamántez, whose mother is at
   work, leaves his mark
        everywhere in the schoolyard,
tosses pages from a thick sheaf of lined
   paper high in the air one by
        one, watches them

catch on the teachers' car bumpers, drift
   into the chalky narrow shade
        of the water fountain.
One last batch, stapled together, he rolls
   tight into a makeshift horn
        through which he shouts

David! and *David, yes!* before hurling it
   away hard and darting across
        Brazos Street against
the light, the little sag of head and
   shoulders when, safe on the other
        side, he kicks a can

in the gutter and wanders toward home.
   David Talamántez believes
        birds are warm blooded,
the way they are quick in the air and
   give out long strings of
        complicated music, different

all the time, not like cats and dogs. For
   this he was marked down in
        Science, and for putting
his name in the wrong place, on the right
   with the date instead of on the
        left with Science

Questions, and for not skipping a line
   between his heading and
        answers. The X's for wrong
things are big, much bigger than
   Talamántez's tiny writing. *Write larger,*
        his teacher says

in red ink across the tops of many pages.
   Messy! she says on others
        where he has erased
and started over, erased and started over.
   Spelling, Language
        Expression, Sentences Using

the Following Words. *Neck. I have a neck*
   name. No! 20's, 30's. *Think*
        again! He's good
in Art, though, makes 70 on Reading
   Station Artist's Corner, where
        he's traced and colored

an illustration from *Henny Penny*. A
   goose with red-and-white striped
      shirt, a hen in a turquoise
dress. Points off for the birds, cloud and
   butterfly he's drawn in
      freehand. *Not in the original*

picture! Twenty-five points off for writing
   nothing in the blank after
      This is my favorite scene
in the book because . . . There's a page called
   Rules. *Listen! Always*
      working! Stay in your seat!

Raise your hand before you speak! No fighting!
   Be quiet! Rules copied from
      the board, no grade,
only a huge red checkmark. Later there is
   a test on Rules. *Listen! Alay*
      ercng! Sast in ao snet!

Rars aone bfo your spek! No finagn! Be cayt!
   He gets 70 on Rules, 10 on
      Spelling. An old man
stoops to pick up a crumpled drawing of
   a large family crowded
      around a table, an apartment

with bars on the windows in Alazán Courts,
   a huge sun in one corner
      saying, *To mush noys!*
After correcting the spelling, the grade
   is 90. *Nice details!* And there's
      another mark, on this paper

and all the others, the one in the doorway
   of La Rosa Beauty Shop, the
      one that blew under
the pool table at La Tenampa, the ones older
   kids have wadded up like
      big spit balls, the ones run

over by cars. On every single page David
   Talamántez has crossed out
      the teacher's red numbers
and written in giant letters, blue ink,
   Yes! David, yes!

Rosemary Catacalos

Mullet

The stupid joy of mullet.

All along the Laguna Madre, mullet

fling themselves into the air for the tiniest sliver

of eternity. Thinking they're flying. Stupid mullet.

Escaping their watery world by three inches, maybe six.

The weight of their tails pulling them back

even as they ascend,

so they never complete an arc,

never cut loose those watery bonds.

The soul of mullet escaping gravity

for a millisecond. And then the dull splash.

Over and over, their short-lived conversions.

All along the Laguna, the plop, plop,

plop of mullet sucked back home.

And again they're at it. As if throwing themselves headlong

up into the abyss. Falling short.

And throwing themselves again. And again the splash.

Their hope and my despair.

The pure illogic of mullet.

A plover flying,
watches this. Then skims the surface,
three inches above water, beak open in
   expectation.
It owns the air. It is the anti-mullet.
A grebe calling, cackling, hooting.
A gull drops headlong
into the water, breaking its glassy plane
on this still day.

Redwing blackbirds, slightly heavier
than a breeze, ride cattails down to the bog.
On shore the cattails are beaten down
   where alligators bed.
Water, sand, air dissolving into each other
at this convergence of the physical universe.
A place of shifting gravities. And again, plop,
the mullet.

Geoff Rips

Progress/Regress
MARCY McCHESNEY

Near Gale

A toss-up. What will
remain of a leaf? A shred
intact? Will a twig snap, or return
to the shape grazing the window?
Will the dog come back?
Will the hinges hold?

Cirrocumulus Undulatus

Eighth, sixteenth notes, brush
strokes. Bristle cone,
thistle head, tic tic.
Slither wisp, scat riff.

Untitled
GAEL STACK

Cirrus Fibratus

The knot's untied. Hair
come loose. Froth of the privet
blousing the grass. Were we
off somewhere? Was there
a memory? A thought?

Altocumulus, Mackerel Sky

Freckled, a dappled thing,
it hasn't yet decided whether
white or blue, fair or foul, coming
or going, riffles, puffballs, dandelion
shreds, a breath, another
river, the current, brimming, gone over.

Wendy Barker

I Know a Thinger Two

Coyotes don't care that you are listening.

If your mule loves you and you are

standing behind her, she will cock

one ear back to listen to your voice as she cocks another forward to

discern whether there are really turkeys

in the small mesquite stand.

Mules are superstitious.

Sometimes bass bite because they are MAD.

It is very important when you are 6 that your 12-year-old brother

bring you back baby snapping turtles

   when he skips school

to go to the river.

It is very important to skip school to go

   to the river.

It is important to catch grasshoppers, beetles, a praying mantis, butterflies,

snakes, lizards, frogs, worms, lightning bugs, and horny toads when you are

young, but you need to let them go.

It's good to know exactly where the moon will rise.

Everything always feels out of place until the Big Dipper is right side up again.

Everything in a pen wants out during the daytime or the nighttime,

depending on its habits.

A family with 3 small children can sleep soundly in their beds for a week

knowing that a 6-foot bull snake is loose in their house.

Of course we dream in color.

When you walk or ride the gently sloping hills of Zavala County, you know

you are at the bottom of what was very recently a shallow, warm ocean.

The whole earth is haunted.

Other people's memories suddenly imprint upon our brains.

People who live without street lights and stop signs and maps

have a better sense of direction and aren't as much afraid when there are no

street lights, stop signs, or maps.

A good horse will get you where you want to go,

but a good mule will enjoy the view.

Your parents should never make you come inside

just because it's dark or raining.

Every house you see on every lonely road, imagine what you would be like

if it had been your home.

The wasp in your hair will probably find its own way out.

Scorpions, tarantulas, and tortoises come out 3 days before a rain.

It was better when the milkman came.

Baby birds push the one they don't like out of the nest

no matter how many times you put it back.

When you are raised under a bowl of sky to horizons in every direction,

mountains can be terrifying.

Owls will answer you at night.

Buzzards eat live baby lambs.

Cattle and sheep graze all facing the same direction. They follow the one

who changes its mind.

Goats love to play king of the mountain, even if the mountain is a rusty car or a tree.

A newborn calf stays in its little bed for at least a week

and does not move until its mother calls it.

Donkeys hoard lawn chairs.

Mules don't like anything to change, even your hairdo.

Everything innocent does its part to save the world.

God doesn't love anybody more.

When you talk to anoles, they will cock their heads and listen to you

before they decide you are not important or interesting.

Half a miracle is noticing. Think of the ones we miss.

Once on a Christmas morning, God gave us a field of thousands of white geese.

Sometimes a redbird at the feeder can save your life.

When you live in Southwest Texas, the migrating monarch butterflies,

orange and gold and lighting on trees, are what God gives you instead of fall.

When a spring is gushing from the side of a hill, surrounded by

maidenhair fern, and a child asks you, "Where does God live?" you say,

"God lives right there." And when the spring dries up and the hole it made

in the hill is surrounded by dead algae and the river is sluggish with scum,

and the child asks, "Where does God live now?"

the answer is, "He lives there still."

To learn where an underground spring feeds into a river, you have

to walk the bottom barefoot.

Ann Alejandro

"THAT SHADOW ON THE GROUND"

Who We Are, Who We Were

Horses in a Perfect Place
BETTIE WARD

an excerpt from CON FLAMA

A PERFORMANCE PIECE

i saw my Ancestors in the eyes of strangers/sitting on the bus. i   collected

their   stories   on   the   bus/in   the   creased

faces   the   bent   backs   the

blistered   hands   the   pieces   of   memory

flickering   neath   the blackbrowntanyellowredwhitebeige   flow

of   skin

the   lilt   and   curve   of   languages   spoken

and   silence   the   music blasting hair wavy kinky straight curly shaved gone

doors swinging open laughter strutting broken yelling fists crumpled smells

somebody's dinner rushing in from streets we passed closed curtains weeping silence

and smiles stepping aboard/i saw myself. who do they look out the window for/wait to

return home from work   who are their Ancestors

i wondered.

i saw my Ancestors in the eyes of strangers/sitting on the bus

i collected their stories/created my story

proudly.

sharon bridgforth

How I learned to love music

My father sits his mornings in the dark,

drinks coffee and listens to his records, waiting

for a singer's weathered mouth to spill wine;

it slicks the floor where the evening's silence falls.

He leans his head against the sounds of guitar strings

and dusty voices that drag low, full with the weight of blue.

The light my mother hangs in the window is not enough

to lure him into waking. She carries lanterns in her hands,

their light grazes my face but sends no sound

thundering across my skin. I hover at the edge of his ritual.

He rocks into the hours' rhythm gently,

jazz riff improvising every new moment.

In the darkness he softly hums my inheritance, waiting

for the chord that will move him into the day.

Vianna Risa Davila

The One Phrase

Once I found my grandmother's
notebook on the kitchen counter.
She had scribbled her name—
Hortencia Gloria Diaz—over and
over again. This from a woman
who can't tell time because the
shapes of numbers are foreign
like black coffee or 99 cent tacos.
This from a woman who demands
grandchildren to read signs on
street corners, signs in her own language.
But somehow, in dark nights, she learned
to write her name, the one phrase
she could read. I imagined
her words twisted on tablet paper,
her ugly, soap-wrinkled fingers
lost between the lines and English lettering.
Digging a piece of lead into white space.
She carves her crooked name until
her hand & arm are sore. Writing, craving
the one phrase, her name.

Radames Ortiz

Galveston Island, 1956

The fenced entrance to the ghost town
of Galveston Ocean Park beckons as fairy light
behind clouds. I don't remember this park,
I wish I did. I wish I could remember crossing
under this arch where a faded mermaid with shells
for breasts floats atop seven plaster waves
breaking in the sky.

R. I. P. Kitty
DANIEL KELLY

I wish I remembered holding Daddy's hand
as we strolled beneath. Or Mother's thick black hair
in the sea mist when we rode the carousel horses,
the Gulf and the moon roaring behind. Or maybe
this carousel would've had giant seahorses with saddles
in the curls of their tails.

Instead I have a ragged souvenir in black & white,
a photograph with scalloped edges, and a year
printed on the side. Like pictures always had
back then. I am nearly six. I squat on the sand,
point to the castle we've built. My straps are loose,
white line snakes over little shoulders.
My face is a smile.

Daddy kneels beside me. He looks like Ricky Ricardo on the beach.
Also he looks like he adores me, which he did. Me?
I look like I'll grow up to be nothing but happy
and normal.

They say every picture tells a story.
What they don't say, is whether the story
is true.

Patty Turner

Why I Envied Boys

Simple enough:
I climbed trees,
found a comfortable niche,
looked through sparse limbs,
to a Panhandle sky
and tried to think boy thoughts.

My eleventh Christmas brought
a Depression-style toolkit,
the basics: a hammer and a saw,
I sawed scrap wood and
dreamed of a ladder to the attic.
Maybe I could make it a room of my own.

Couldn't deliver groceries
for Mr. Balbo
because I was a girl.
The insult was attending
a girls' school. I was in trouble
often for my good ideas,
nuns could not conceive a boxing team.

All of this changed when I learned
to dance. Well, almost.
If I had been a boy,
I could have chosen my partner.

Naomi Stroud Simmons

Cloud

*If you are a poet, you will see clearly that there is a cloud
floating in this sheet of paper.*

—THICH NHAT HANH

Before you became a cloud, you were an ocean, roiled and
murmuring like a mouth. You were the shadow of a cloud crossing over a field of tulips. You were the tears of a man who cried
into a plaid handkerchief. You were a sky without a hat. Your
heart puffed and flowered like sheets drying on a line.

And when you were a tree, you listened to trees and the tree
things trees told you. You were the wind in the wheels of a red
bicycle. You were the spidery *María* tattooed on the hairless arm
of a boy in downtown Houston. You were the rain rolling off the
waxy leaves of a magnolia tree. A lock of straw-colored hair
wedged between the mottled pages of a Victor Hugo novel. A
crescent of soap. A spider the color of a fingernail. The black nets
beneath the sea of olive trees. A skein of blue wool. A tea saucer
wrapped in newspaper. An empty cracker tin. A bowl of blueberries in heavy cream. White wine in a green-stemmed glass.

And when you opened your wings to wind, across the punched-
tin sky above a prison courtyard, those condemned to death and
those condemned to life watched how smooth and sweet a white
cloud glides.

Sandra Cisneros

Summers in the Country

FOR TINO VILLANUEVA

Summers in the country, I was the city boy
up from Dallas to visit the farm, up to visit
up to visit up to no good up to corrupt (those
old ladies said behind their curtains) those
country girls those twelve-year-old cowgirls
who snuck beers behind the rodeo stands and
those boys who talked about which cows were
best who wondered what the heck I found so
interesting about the damn graveyard and
why did I always have a damn book with me
and was I writing down notes to give their
damn mothers or what.
       Summers in the country
I was Huckleberry looking for Jim and a river
I was Woody looking for a song and glory I was
Meg trying to tesser and Davy trying to trap
the perfect coon for the perfect hat and trying
to get it all down on a backpocket steno pad
taking shorthand on life and getting curiouser
and curiouser about how my parents survived
this damn town.
       Summers in the country I drove
grandpa's air-conditioned tractor while the field hands
bent double down the long rows sometimes singing
chopping cotton always sweating every one of them

a philosopher of labor a poet of the machete
an Odysseus making his way back home every
one of them knowing more about the land than I
ever would in a lifetime of summers in the country.

Bryce Milligan

Barton Springs
Malou Flato

Migrant Birds

Swept by invisible brooms,
black birds, like words on a page,
specks of spilt ground
pepper blown in the wind,
much bigger though,
tightly—not randomly—
change course all
together, but not
altogether at the same,
exact moment.

So-called "junk" birds
swim the skies, come north
for a while to make a life.
Ready now, they once again
become fluid spice, do their
instinctual dance, moved
not by whim, but fancy anyway,
and the hot pepper blows
home to southern climes,
seasoning skies elsewhere for a time.

Moumin Manzoor Quazi

There Have Always Been Trees Outside My Window

World stop.
Trees you tell the world
to stop.
Trees you give birth
to everything
remind the world
of its deathbed.
Trees show me
the edges of
my feet, feet
hedge yourselves in
don't let the world
cut you, not now.

World stop.
Stop cutting.
Stop growing.
The trees will
never forgive you.

Ben Judson

Coming Back into the Sun

Could it be yours,
that shadow on the ground?
Strangely alone.
Vulnerable. New
and pale as a seedling
just plucked from dense
shade.

You shrink from this
reminder. Cautiously
study its edges,
sharply unique, exactly
drawn to fit, too clear
and well-defined
to deny. It is you.

Remember when you were a child
how far your shadow seemed to go?
How you filled all
of its long possibilities?
Now you think you can't
but you move.
Timorously, at first.
Then with abandon.
You know this shadow
needs you.

If you dance, it will.

Wendy Dimmette

Thirteen

The boy in the baggy shorts
tosses back his forelock before he shoots.

When the corners of the cracked court darken,
he saunters in.

Six months ago he was at home
in her kitchen, chocolate
milk on his chin, handicapping the Bulls,
describing the new kid in algebra.

So much a part of her rooms he was
a chair, the thermometer.
"Mom it's hot." Underfoot.

In July he talked
about baseball. Now he reads
alone in the evenings. He has nothing to
    say.

Before he goes out, the boy
puts on his Spurs jersey.

His Mother has washed it
until it is thin as milk.

Wendy Taylor Carlisle

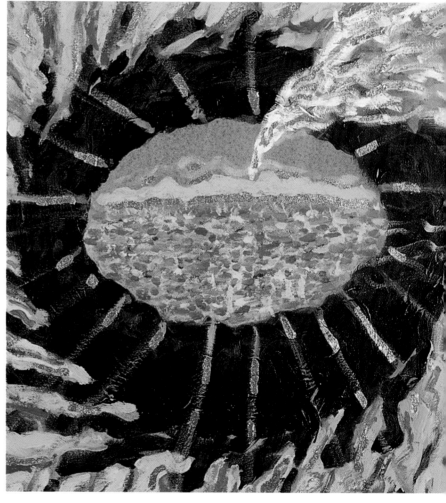

Smoke
PEDRO LUJÁN

Wearing the River

Skirting sandstone boulders, reclimbing
the hills we had switchbacked across,
we were finally tramping home, and with
the edges of our heels we tattooed paths
of quarter moons down a dry creekbed
then another set across the half-mud top
of a dried-out stock tank, and slopping up
onto the weedy bank, we kept wandering—
no one in a hurry to get back to town
Zigzagging mesquite-crowded pasture,
we flushed cottontails, lizards and finches

We were making our labyrinthine way
over, around and through short walls
of prickly pear, catclaw and spiderwebs,
thorns snagging our Levi's, thorns nicking
socks and shirts and arms—the scent
of dust a bit like the fragrance of blood
rising into our nostrils now: we were
the river we'd been horsing around in,
the wash of gypsum salt and red clay silt
had dried—it was cracking with each step,
and sulphurous, the syrup smell of oil
drifted in with the scent of dust—
a slough pit nearby, and we'd almost

walked in it: we'd been watching a scissortail
warting a hawk in the currents above us—
a funky music on the wind: a pumpjack's
squeak and sputter-pop, its brass tongue
bobbing into the cored-out earth—the river
still with us, layered on clothes and skin

James Hoggard

So Much Depends

How like an alchemist's chant the red wheelbarrow poem
seemed in tenth grade. Mrs. Morgan, with her new novels
had already been taken by Debbie Jackson's mother before
the school board for those nasty books little Debbie
had been forced to read. I remember Stuart Tackitt saying
he didn't understand the mother's fury, "Hell, Debbie
would have been the girl on the elevator with Holden."
But the school board did not know Debbie did tricks
after ballgames and did not want our impressionable minds
reading about sin. So Mrs. Morgan did not return
the next year, but it did not matter. She had already
taught us about the red wheelbarrow. We were the white
chickens, and all that depending got into our thinking.
We were unreliable things, moving in and out of the school yard.
Even chickens are different after a storm.

Edward E. Wilson

Now, That Is Summer

The day makes a map of disappearing,
frenzied rumor of hummingbird
between how we see and are seen.

Last night around the fire
a voice said, you know this conversation
only seems to be based in reality.

Most days I only seem to be based in reality.

A cook stacks sweaty potato after potato
into a pyramid on the counter
but sees only peels
limp and smudged at his feet.
Or does he?

The day makes a map of disappearing
and the ants need a bridge
for carrying crumbs twice their size.
That too is a life.

The blue hammock closes her eyes, sighs
and longs for a different one
boat of water, birth sling, crack in earth
swallowing my back.

There are moments I pretend I am popcorn
swelling to fourteen times my original size
and nobody ever looks surprised.

All I want is to watch an old lady's hand
reach through our fence for a fist
of rosemary, the spice
of remembrance. How far

must she carry it? How far
must it carry me?

Just now sputtering lines of laughter arch
from the neighbor's sprinkler
and pairs of shiny brown legs begin
their pedal through then back around

our street in endless circles.

Someone looks up and says, now that is
    summer.
Someone looks and says poor kids.
Someone says faster, faster.

Jenny Browne

Sweet Dreams

Voices fade as he walks
into them. He hears his name
in the air above him, passed
from parents to guests
and back to him like a ball.
The plates have faces. In his
father's he sees his own.
The candle's shadow is talking
and laughing with the wall.
There are kind questions
for him, shared silences he hears
himself speak into: he blinks,
whispers to the floor,
a small fist blooms with years
he's stored in fingers. Somewhere

in their watches are the hours
he can't enter. In awkward
pauses some stare into his sleep.
A red-nailed finger slowly circles
the rim of a glass, but the red
bell of wine won't sing.
They look at him and smile.
His mother stands, her hand enclosing
his. His father's cheek cuts
into his kiss. The hardwood floor
shines eyes of light. The dark
doorway is the wall's yawn.
He walks into their wishes.

Christian Wiman

Dream of Texas
DEBORAH MAVERICK KELLEY

Almost Asleep

I am close to my bed. I am close to my book.

I am close to my chair. And my silence lights the room.

There is no other real joy but this:

to feel as if a glass of milk were warming

inside one's stomach,

to pick out familiar tunes in Tchaikovsky

and hum along,

to wish the best for the world without me.

For I'm elsewhere, about to enter sleep.

All the lullabies I ever heard beckon me.

All the fairy tales and nursery rhymes

my mother—she was forever at my bedside—

filled me with return like a messenger.

And I say to the children of the world:

Take comfort. Someday, you, too,

will treasure your moments of sleep—

even more than your parents promised.

Someday the pony who visits you

will be your companion again.

Ken Fontenot

Black-Eyed Susans

Me
trying on makeup for the first time.
My dress is psychedelic
and breasts nonexistent, dark buds
beginning to hum.
Them
huddled with frightened glances
in pool table yards,
crowded by dahlias and their toe-roots,
by asters turning smeared faces toward heaven.
Me
after the party and boyfriend breakup,
mascara charcoaled onto
pillows and sleeves.
Them
blown by the heat of barbeques and families,
before frost exhumes their pungent light.
Me

in another life named Sue or Susie or Susannah,
picking bee-colored suns
with only You in a field of
Them.

Carla Hartsfield

Ulcerville
RAINEY

mobile home still life

yards and yards of *Fleur de Lis*–patterned paper wall to
wall over a   breath of wood, pressed wood, plywood,
wood paneling

       the flowers supposed to excuse this excuse for a
home   our tinning promise
there is an island in the kitchen, a built-in bar, the
windows slide open and shut guillotine style, face a
road that waits to leave,

          to feel to the tips of its extremities
the breakfast nook is lined with a wallpaper of
vegetables and the names of different dishes;
*la soupe aux haricots, le potage de legumes, la soupe de
jour* which tells me, once, someone else wanted out of
here, sat at the breakfast table and wanted to curl her
toes underneath a table at a cafe along the Seine
                             but

I fear I have finally assumed the life of this place

if you wanted to paint a mobile home still life   it
would be me at the counter or in front of the tv set or
at a sink full of dishes   staring out the kitchen window   watching the clouds pass us right by   it would
be me   polyfiber under Plexiglas   wrapped
in *Fleur de Lis* tissue stuffed   in a tin box

Sheila S. Hatch

Something Important

When I mastered waiting
I loved being alone
inside the waiting
and the waiting
inside being alone.

I didn't know what I was waiting for
or why I loved being alone, just that
the deep Zen spearmint breath of
    timelessness
taught me how to hold back the delicious
and polish that stone with my mind
until I could accept the world
for what it was, impervious,
because I contained it.

And I wasn't anything yet.
I was a boy, water swirling
through water, which made waiting seem
like a wise decision, made me feel important,
though I looked like a battered contender
who could splatter chaos with a flight of
    thought.

And I still don't know what's happening,
only that when I finally go it'll all go on
    without me
in a form I can't imagine, and I accept that,
despite not feeling right, despite forgetting
what I'm waiting for, because there's a
    wisdom in me
I recognize and prize, whether or not I'm
    right.

Jack Myers

Of Age

Even at eighteen, having held the reins
of the sun god's chariot, having ridden Pegasus
zenith to zenith and not tumbled, burning,
having thrown our heads back and laughed
at all divine warnings, I shivered
when Mark and I opened the screen door
to his grandmother's rented house and entered
the dark kitchen smelling of bacon grease
and dirt cellar and saw Mama Rose
through the portal to the sitting room
and sleeping porch, not even rocking
in the upholstered chair she brought from the farm,
not even spitting snuff into the tin can
deadened with newsprint.
Neither Mark nor I could cross into that room,
neither of us able to ask for pecan pie
and a glass of milk, nor strong enough
to flip on the light. We waited for her to rise
from her underworld throne, wave her wand,
return spring and summer. She permitted us
only her profile, her pronouncement: "It goes so fast."
Even then I knew it was what we had come to hear.

Robert Fink

Dancing Bodies, Heat Wave

As a kind of droughtsong,
the willow curled her leafy

flutterings into question marks
littering the lawn lemon-pale.

I moved like a stagehand after,
leaf-blower making a loud sad music.

I went to a pond and fed a handful
of day-old bread to a few ducks,

their tails rhythmic as always.
Their eyes inscrutable as a poet's.

I watched a few cars collide
on heat-slick asphalt, heads slam

glass, mouths form screams. Later,
I shaved my dog. Now, in my lap

here on the couch, he meditates
with me on the meanings of the Sun.

Enigmas of the Sun. He's imagining
water, I imagine: that backyard pool

he'll linger in under the old pecans
shading him, a few rib bones he's buried

there beside it. I can see only
the ancient stone, *la luna*, reflecting,

reflected: leaf, sign, fruit, work, creature,
music, madness, friend-in-dreamland.
   The god.

The dead bodies and the living bodies, all
dancing together, but the strange angles

of the light rising and falling, curving and
deflecting off the silence inside them.

Daniel Durham

Untitled
YU CHA PAK

San Antonio Snapshots

Painting summer
as a child
the sun was often yellow.

Dusty boots
at the front door
a cricket tries one on.

Coming and going
the only road
in town.

Sparrows gather
outside the cantina
for a bite to eat.

Michael A. Moore

Heat

When we first arrived, nothing
seemed to be growing, the brown
a kind of final color. Even cottonwoods
in their dust and tortured bark were another
form of rock. I flinched from the sky, trying
to find room, that summer of cracked skin

Waiting for Rain
BILLY HASSELL

where the river used to be. Dried grass,
the real frontier, blew white across my brow,
and all through the drought's expected
deprivations, we spoke less and less.
I rubbed my dry face until I drew blood.

One day something alive at my feet sent up
a pale green smell. Aged water and sun.
Quail suddenly gathered themselves
from the sand, thrumming with purpose,
and then I noticed miniature leaves
close to the ground making secret cover.
"Sage," you told me later, when I opened my palm.

Sunset began to pick out the dunes
earlier each afternoon. They bloomed peach,
rose, before their shadows spread over the valley
into one element. Water. It stroked our house until
the windows filled with ordinary light.
And every evening the neighbor's gentle horses
paced their corral, in the darkness, waiting
for their hay. Every evening they were
hungry. Then they were happy.

Leslie Ullman

Underfoot

Because it was August in Texas
and I was sweating an uphill trail,
waving away clusters of gnats
that clung like gold dust to the heat

I nearly stepped upon the head of a long black snake.
Leaping aside, I wanted to prod the harmless
snake with a stick, make it ripple silent as a shadow:
we both held our ground.

Because I had come so close to stepping upon
that snake, I recalled all the snakes
that had appeared before me—*the coral snake*
sliding down our driveway at night

while I walked barefoot beneath the stars;
the rattlesnake, coiled in our garage,
its high-pitched sound hard to hear amid the chanting
katydids, how we hosed and hosed it

until it surrendered the cool cement for underbrush;
the stillness of a king snake idling across the warm road,
when I tapped the tail it turned alongside itself
and headed straight for me;

the small yellow snake with brown
railroad tracks marking its spine
that I lifted with ice prongs from our living
room; the water moccasin

that glided beside me in the Little Blanco River,
how I slapped the water to discourage it
from coming any closer—with all these snakes
in mind, I bowed to the one before me

watched it flow toward the cedars.
Striding home, I saw snakes everywhere:
a stick flicked its tongue among the boulders,
black electrical tape once coiled in a dusty heap

slipped into an asphalt crevice,
even the belt around my husband's waist
unhooked its copper mouth, wriggled down his leg,
and claimed a crack in our kitchen floorboards.

Cyra S. Dumitru

Woman Waiting for Heat-Relief Assistance Overcome by Record-Breaking Heat

I couldn't stand no more,
even though I wore soft shoes.

We got in line when the sun was coming up.
People kept saying it was going to rain,

as if they were blind.

I wore these soft white shoes,
but I would stand ankle deep in mud right now

for some rain. My friend

tells me they're giving away window units and money
here. But I couldn't make it to the door.

Been standing out here since daybreak,
up and down the line people kept saying, *rain*.

I sweated through my best blouse,
wanted to look nice once I got inside.

But I couldn't stand no more,
even though I wore these soft white shoes.

Mary Agnes Dalrymple

Nearing 100°

I do not need
to be in an air-conditioned
room in the afternoon.

I just need to know
that it exists.

Robert Trammell

What It Is
to Be Happy

I will ride a horse into the sea,
the sea lace and blue wind,
the wind foaming about us.
Every ship enters its harbor.

Valerie Crosswell

Sardines with Self-Portrait
DANIEL KELLY

The Trees Greet the Rain

You were gone so long the soil shrank back from our trunks.
Many of us fell, our roots having nothing
to hold on to. Finding no water, our taproots
struggled down until they tasted damp
at the planet's molten core.

                          You have come back,
as you said you would. We need you no longer.
We fear neither termite nor chainsaw. We have drunk something
immortal, the Earth told us, and we have a new name:
Iron. You can come or go as you will.
What can you do to us?

Bruce Tindall

"IS THIS FOREVER, OR WHAT?"

Pairs of People

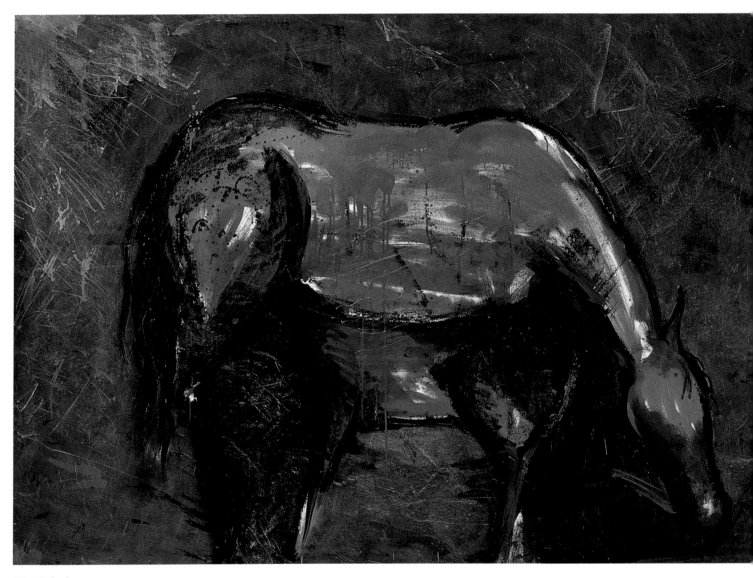

Untitled
JULIA MCLERNON

Mystery

I look at the pairs of people. Some
mystery contained between them.
The hand inserted in a pocket
for money before the other asks.
The careful pause, however slight,
for the other's rounded belly
when there's no room
for both to fit with ease
through a narrow doorway
or between a heavy chair and its table.

What is the glue holding people
together? It can't be passion.
I don't believe it's curiosity.
Surely not beauty, or lies,
or mere habit. If I knew
I'd give it to you and to me
like a bitter dose out of a blue bottle
to seal us together
to make us one
for a blessed eon.

Sarah Cortez

The Shirt

My girls wear their friends' clothes,
and half of their clothes stay
at somebody else's house.
Once in a while a colorful shirt
turns up—doesn't belong to anyone.
One girl wears it, the whole day blessed
by the colors of that surprising shirt.

Del Marie Rogers

Love Handout for the Gorgeous to Give the Stricken

STRICKEN: READ THIS

Remember
if you fall
in love with me
to keep on falling
past me,
right into the abyss,
and keep on falling
right through the abyss
until you come out
the other side and see
that the sun
is just hydrogen
burning off in space.

(Maybe I have a family already, maybe I
have a wonderful life already and want you for a friend, maybe you're
the wrong species! There are many good reasons I could or should
not fall in love with you—and who wants to fall where you are headed?)

Fall past, and joy will be in your nostrils
just because you breathe; and clouds and sky

over trees and flowers will not look like me.
You will be glad they do not look like me.

Fall until you are a person
who can walk on earth alone—

So much of love is a dream!
I know you knew.

Oh, and the sun is really not
just hydrogen melting. But

go ahead, pretend this is so for a while.
And the sun will return to the sky.

Ignacio R. Magaloni

Santo Niño Perdido,
Rey de Los Angeles de Portiuncula
DAVID ZAMORA CASAS

Strike Zone

If, for example,
you aim at me,
wind up
and throw—
at the right
height
and speed—
and
I'm paying
attention
and functioning
at all—
you're going
to get
smashed.

A hardball,
well thrown,
could get hit
out of the ballpark
on a good day,
if I'm
paying attention
that is—

Otherwise
I might walk,
steal a base,
slide home.

Home is where I live.
A hardball
into that strike zone
is very likely
to get smashed.

Susan Bright

The Summer Her Family Moved to Houston

Don't ask, Uncle Bill scolded.
You don't want to know. Oh, but I did,
Aunt Emma bursting with secrets
I should know. What happens when a body rots,

when cancer eats the lungs? What did he mean,
exquisite pain? Nine, I had felt fire
when I swallowed with my tonsils gone—
saved by a fire brigade of nurses

with ice cream. I had seen dead pigs,
found my brother's old dog stiff
behind the barn. What could be worse
than watching Barbara ride off

in her family's packed station wagon,
waving from the tailgate and weeping,
leaving for Houston a thousand miles away?
Oh, if anything would ever be worse

than watching their vacant house for hours
across the road, no one to ride with
across a mile of meadow to the muddy Brazos,
Barbara forever gone, I had to know.

Walt McDonald

At Sixteen

I walked under a fire escape splashed with gasoline.
    I walked past a sweatshop buried in a warehouse
where dozens of women were sewing garments.
    I got a job as a waiter in a downtown restaurant.

I walked past a sweatshop buried in a warehouse.
    My father lent me the car on Saturday nights.
I waited on tables in a downtown restaurant
    and ate in the kitchen with the other waiters.

My father lent me the car on Saturday nights.
    I took my girlfriend to the beach for parties.
I ate in the kitchen with the other waiters.
    Everyone laughed at my enormous appetite.

I took my girlfriend to the beach for parties.
    She wanted to get married, get pregnant.
Everyone laughed at my enormous appetite.
    I wanted her so much I thought I'd die of it.

She wanted to get pregnant, get married.
    I wrote a poem about a closing steel door.
I wanted her so much I thought I'd die of it.
    I got a job in a warehouse next to a factory.

I wrote a poem about a steel door closing.

     I walked under a fire escape splashed with gasoline.

I took orders in a warehouse next to a factory

     where dozens of women were feeding machines.

Edward Hirsch

After I Bought Her 2 New Dresses and Blue Contact Lenses
VINCENT VALDEZ

Giant, Red Hibiscus

I wish you were here waiting with me in my mother's garden.
The early morning sunlight has splintered
through the fence, has every leaf glittering.

I am waiting for the giant, red face of the hibiscus to open.

And I would like to watch you watch the hibiscus
in early morning,
how it changes from some seemingly red, dead-looking thing
into the most beautiful bloom on earth.

I'm sorry, I forgot. I meant the second most beautiful thing.

How many times have you said
that I never share anything with you,
that I never tell you what's important to me?
Well, here it is. The hibiscus, I mean.

When I saw it yesterday for the first time I remembered difficulty.
And I wanted you to see it.

I wanted us to watch something open and not be afraid.

Travis Ian Smith

Mr. Confusion

Hey, You! Mr. Confusion!
Ducking from an imaginary dive-bombing bird.
Looking like a wide-eyed lost owl.

Where are You going, man?
Hey, watch it!
You almost hit your head on yourself.
But I can sympathize, yeah I can.

See, I've been tossed at sea more than once.
Lost in a fog more than that.
Looking like a fool all the time
Or at least it seems that way.

But You know, we always find our
way back somehow, we do.
Ow!! Stubbed your toe again?
Ouch! I felt that too!

This way or that?
Which way are You heading?
Oh! Oh! Crossroads ahead.
Well, good luck!
Hey, wait!
You forgot your head, man!

Joseph H. Garcia

Silent Voices
SCOTTIE PARSONS

What

Is this forever, or what? I asked
a few weeks into summer, the sky
had widened and I needed to know
right then, while we were parked

in the lot behind the waterslide
where nothing grew, just us
and dust, and our little city buzzed
in the valley, a dozen or so roads

cut into it. It'd be nice to go back
to speaking so easily. *Just ask*,
the sky suggested and in reply the boy
turned the key in the ignition

and drove us back into town, along
the same streets, which led one
into the next and were measured only
as we passed over them.

Carrie Fountain

Black Swallowtail

On the telephone
to break up with you

      when the chrysalis
      splits
      damp wings unwilting

You plead
I wait

      The wings dry and brighten
      to orange   moonwhite and turquoise
      too big for the tangled
      amber crust

      It climbs like a little colt up my white sleeve
      stilts and wingtails quivering
      to the thump of my heart

Who's weak? I ask   carrying the phone

      and the bug
      out the back door
      putting it leg by leg
      on the doorframe

It curls its flowersucking tongue
A gust comes   it blows away
                      on blue-lit wings
to eringo's
                      silver candelabra
umbelliferous
                      like my dill
autumn's magenta nursery

You sniff thickly
those pale tears must roll like beads
down your thin white skin

Don't look for answers live the question
                      the poet wrote

I hook the phone and start your way
                      I'm the other wing of this unknown.

Barbara Orlovsky

*Black swallowtail larvae feed on carrot, parsley, and related plants.
*Eringo is a prickly member of the parsley family, whose
 flowerheads and leaves turn bright violet in the fall.

Vibrating Crystal

Got a letter some time back
said they had my one-hundred-dollar
Four-Million-Year-Old
Vibrating Crystal
and that they were holding it
in their Security and Safekeeping Div.
in Safe Deposit Vault # 565
under my personal registration file 37A
at the World Crystal Center
at 382 Main St.
in Hackensack, NJ.
(I won't bother you with the zip code
but I have it
if you need further verification.)

They say that it has been
gemologically classified and
is a power stone treasure,
a precious icy Clear Quartz Crystal
certified similar to crystals on display
at New York's famed Museum of Natural History
and the Smithsonian Institute in Washington, D.C.
And it has one Natural Energy Point.
They said to keep the Ownership Certificate enclosed
with my other Personal Valuables
and that they will send my Ownership Title Papers

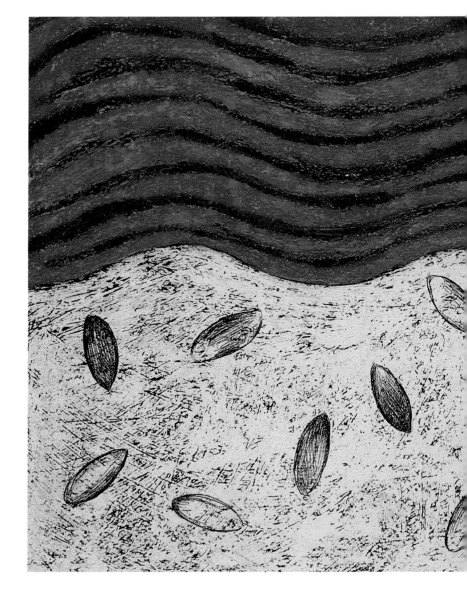

Sow
PAULA OWEN

when I tell them to send me my crystal.
(I have twenty-one days to respond.
After that they'll take my number
out of their data bank file.)
They keep saying in the letter
I already own the crystal,
and that the $19 I'm to send them
covers shipping, jewelry handling,
insurance, and certification processing.

Further, if I return the enclosed form
within 3 days   8 days   15 days
(eight days was checked),
I will get free a special edition of
Crystal Power News which tells me
how to get all the benefits
from my Power Stone possession,
updated reports on scientific developments,
and how people use Crystal
to gain money, love, and happiness.

They don't know I already have
all the money and love I want
and that their letter has given me
all the happiness I need for the moment.

Richard Sale

Apothecary, in Time of Joy

Give your old love letters over
to the fire. There is nothing
that can come of them now.

If you keep them, though, take the praises
and petal them together, in such a way
that *I love you* simply becomes *you are loved*,

and all the kisses you collected become
radium as the Curies knew it:
light rested in the palms,

fingertips touching,
a mystery housed
in hands.

Regard the sun as a rare thing
that has come out for you. Use
words like *phoenix* and *resurrection*, and believe them.

Be with the cherry trees in the courtyard
in spring, the Japanese Rorschach
of pink and white on the skeletons

you have been avoiding all winter.
Pick your heart out of the branches,
and let it rest. There.

Phil West

Bagpiper in the Park

A lone bagpiper was playing in the park,
somewhere in the trees
with a high melody above a low drone
that struck a bone in my breast.

Everyone on the path commented
about the strange music for our morning.
Because of its whining call we were all ready
to join the ranks of some great cause,
certain that something righteous
should no longer be downtrodden.

People removed their earphones.
Deer were neither frightened nor curious
and no dogs howled in answer.
Everything listened. It was the great fact
of that morning in the park. It was as if
the park had something to say
and had finally found a voice.

Margie McCreless Roe

Found Things

I stumble from room to room
lost like a young wild boy
whose pockets once were stuffed
with marbles and frogs,
foreign coins and knotted string,
a pocket knife and a hollow
silver locket, but now has
discovered his clothing empty.

He searches under his bed, behind
bookcases, in the far back
reaches of his black closet
where he sometimes hides. Nothing.
Where could it all have gone?
Vanished as strangely and miraculously
as it all had come to him—
found things, gifts and thefts.

This has happened so often.
So this time before he takes
his papers and paints and throws
them to the floor, before he shouts
so that everyone in the distant
corners of his house comes running,
this time he stops and imagines
a pile of lost things someone else

will find: unasked-for treasures,
coins from places unheard of, string
from kites set free, an empty locket
once held close to a heart in love.
I wander the rooms of my house now,
not searching, not angry, not
even hopeful. I am merely ready
for the miracle of found things.

Lyman Grant

The Martins

MARGIE CRISP

Little Lies

Your arm looked as big as
a rolled roast.
We didn't have anything
to talk about,
And time was sliding away
so fast.
I'm sorry, I
just didn't know how
to say it.
There was so much pretending
going on, I didn't know
where to put the truth.

I just see that arm resting on
the seat of the car
next to me,

and the two of us
opening and closing
our empty mouths.

Fran Hillyer

Big Detail #2
AARON PARAZETTE

Our Time

"from all other ages how little has come to me"

—W. S. Merwin

our time together is all we can
know with any small confidence
what we ourselves have ever seen
as ourselves in the time we look
called life which is the time to know
know well as only time can be
known which is ourselves in time
now and now only when we only are
ourselves and time if time can ever be
is real as you and me together now
calling ourselves ourselves with confidence

F. J. Schaack

Inner Lids

Imagine each of us
our own language, diction
and rhythms, singular
turns of phrase.

Next, the dog
her eyes upturned black flesh
of inner lids, will rise
from the couch
place a paw on my shoulder
the other on yours
and in quiet tones
not hushed but nearly so
will explain finally
the unholy machinations
of this universe
how the world formed
what love is
why every endeavor, ever.

David Ray Vance

The Levee

A six-banded racer makes its way through
Open grass and scattered thistles; Follows
Tortured mesquite posts along the sun-parched
Soil to my home: A ranch, with boarded
Windows, dilapidated trailers and pens of
Tools in disuse. This is a place owned by
Invisible souls designated by names on fine-threaded
Paper and middle men set on haunches—sweating
With the slightest spoken word. This is the ranch,
Not our ranch; Hogs and steer walk within firmly
Placed enclosures; Crooked signs on cul-de-sacs
Summon haggard grackels filching ruby reds from
Forbidden stalks. This is a garden, not our
Garden, where mangy hounds are called wolves and
Infirm cackling chicks are golden chanticleers.
Where the burden of our day's long labor
Funnels down to pits of obese men and
False men—colored, but not colored—knowing
The ways and spittling in our faces on Sunday
Afternoons. (They go to church—St. Mary's—
And shake the hands of our fathers with diluted
Speech and broken vowels from mass an hour before.)

This is the Rio Grande, thirsty and forgotten;

It gargles plastic bags and wading pancake-colored

Interlopers—our brothers and our enemies—while

Green jays perch on cottonwood boughs and speak

The word to no one but our own.

The great black eagle (is that what it is?) sits on

A red background with geometric wings and bespeaks

My world; middle men proclaim my world. The similar

Toads who hold the cow and hen and pig hold the

Banner and proclaim the world, extol the sickle and

Rapier. I believe in nothing in particular when

The road leads to my home—a small shack—and tears

A wound in my lower right chest, where the hand was

Placed and my palm was shook, after mass. When I

Can hear them besmirch my every move with a tilt of

The pen. This is the place where my children were born,

Where they will live and die without raising

The voice we know nothing of,

And never will.

Rodney Gomez

The Angus Martyr

Fifty years past, he had watched a cow drown itself
rather than be herded into a pasture bordered by rusty fences.
A black Angus pledged herself to the ancient mud
of the brown Rio Grande while the boy yelled
"come back" from far away across the dry land.

The cow had come from Mexico where there were no
fences and the thing went down into water preferring
the regions without wire. As a man, the boy
would remember often that sad Angus martyr,
he would rise up out of his sleep with the suspicion
that miles away cows were lowing at the moon in pain,
he would fall back only to dream of cows,
how nightly they broke through fences like a part of him
with their stupid bodies and enormous heads.
He would have a son born with a long, furry tail
like a cow's, and together they would build fences
because fences are the sufferings that must be built.
After a day of stretching barbed wire across cedar
the boy that became the man would drink black coffee
while his son out in the pasture would call
to the cows to come lick at the salt blocks,
calling with a deep animal sound stirring in his lungs.

The fences went out like lines that never finish
and every night some beast would try that tension
letting the fences ring, post to post across the land.
And every night the man would tell his son
about the tail he had been born with, its gentle fur
when they cut it off just after the child's birth,
and about the great black head of that Angus bobbing up
out of the Rio Grande, black hide glistening with mud.

John Phillip Santos

*Green Pears
and Tree Frog*
ANDREA PEYTON

squirrel's hands

my aunt used to say she wanted to come back
a tiger in her next life
my father said he would return an eagle
my mother preferred something small and simple
a sparrow

grandmother crossed over without ever saying
but recently I have spotted her
she is a squirrel living close by
she measures acorns that resemble thimbles
and raises mast to scissor teeth

already she senses
            the heartbeats
                        of life continuing
                                    beyond her

when she sewed, the exact gestures of my grandmother's hands
were like a squirrel's examining hickories and walnuts.
she did not cut thread so long it tangled,
for she knew its umbilical weight

the cloth in her hands acquired vibrato,
each stitch pulsed with apt and supple care
she did not have to say
I will return a squirrel
she knew I would recognize her hands

Mobi Warren

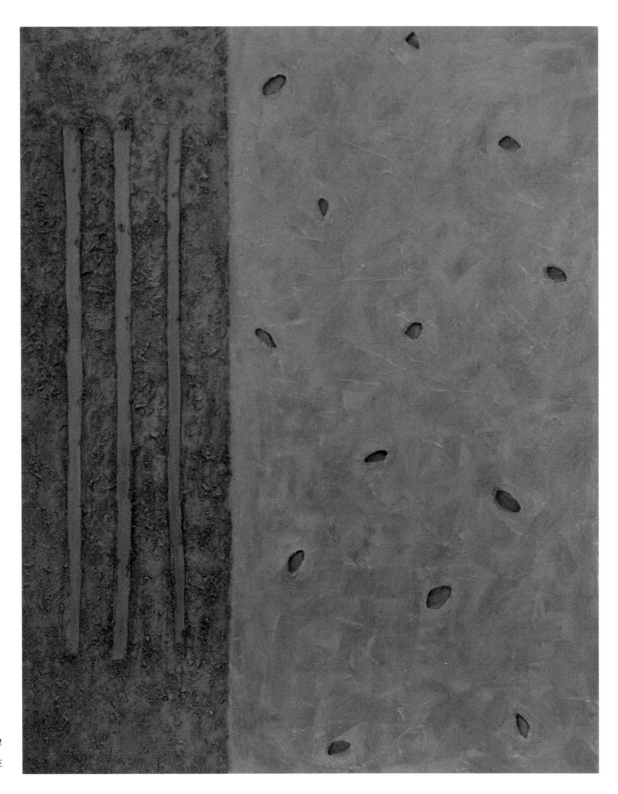

Red Constellation
REGINALD ROWE

Rodney
OMAR RODRIGUEZ

New West

wide spiritual country
moving is standing still
days disappear
a peace the soul sacrifices
before moving
onward in distance

people get lost here
why do you think
there are mobile homes
where the buffalo once roamed?

old man cowboy
a rocking horse
who would have thought
to watch him walk
back and forth

Trey Moore

River in the Dark
—ALONG THE SAN MARCOS RIVER

All green gone. Trees. The river,
we remember, winds through
the trees—they follow it down
the hills. The moon gives enough
light tonight to see light upon
the current. Fireflies above—
their spark stumbles too
on the surface of the water.

At the sound of a river
the body chills, awake from
summer, shocked open. At
the mention of motion, the mind
accepts another way. It is willing
to go past the last trails, streets
of the city. The river is not
what we thought we wanted.

Beside water, the dark is
never dark. Night keeps moving.
Whatever falls away feels right—
here where no stone is silent.

Steve Wilson

Mitote of the Mud-Dauber

Home is not far, little mother
            Home is everywhere
Earth is there
Earth is here

Build a house, little mother,
Of earth and rain,
With care, little mother, with care,
In air and sun

A broken house lets out the sun
            Hum and dance and wall it in

A broken house lets in the moon
            Hum and dance and wall it out

Home is not far, little mother
            There is no wandering
Earth is here
Water is here

Earth is everyone's cud
            Hum and dance and taste it again
It still tastes like home

John Igo

"LOVING THE SKY"

Personal Histories, Beneath It

Dead Grasses
JULIE BOZZI

Making Room

My mother envied the small women,
the ones with bones like blades
of grass, bones
blown thin as wineglass stems,
airy and fragile. Even their shadows
took up less space on the sidewalk,
making more room
for love. *I've always been big-boned*,
she'd say, a testimony
to her genetic misfortune, a woman
in a long line of women, tall and athletic
with strong hands and shoulders.
She could work for hours in the garden,
bent over the tomatoes
and squash fattening there
beside her in the sun.
And so each summer
the emptying-out began,
a grapefruit half for breakfast,
bowl after bowl of cabbage soup.
With the beautiful excess of the Saints,
my Catholic-reared mother
tried to shed flesh
like the chickens she boiled
for dumplings and broth.
Edgy, her eyes cleaned out,
miraculous and holy,
she'd descend the scales each morning
with her body
a little more defeated.
She'd cling to me, her firstborn son,
whose small bones
were strung together
like wind chimes, singing
a love song
of what she wanted
to be, singing
all through the house.

Bruce Snider

Deer Kiln

The front porch screens are hung with water
  droplets
and beyond the bluff's edge a buzzard drifts
in an ocean-sky of mist.
The house floats rudderless.
From shrouded trees a thunderous crack.

The men stomp in from the morning's hunt,
proud, a little pale, in muted light.
One of them, my son who left before dawn,
his hands unstained,
returns cradling the still warm gun.

"I'm sorry, Mom, about the deer," he says.
I hug him and his shoulders curve the same
only not as softly as before,
as though he'd passed through a place
that only I could see—

a kiln of sorts
set up to fire a boy into a man
harshly by the squeezing
of a metal moon
and the bursting forth of power.

I stay close to the cabin
avoiding the color and smell beyond
while fog thickens around us
obscuring even the outline
of the hill next to ours,

searching for a power
more subtle than a rifle shot
that can mingle spirits in the fog
both men and deer
turning them finally to the same dust.

Patricia Spears Bigelow

Blessing

Resurrection. Ascension of bone
against bone. There is something that
   clatters
like fangs strung together on twine
about my neck. Black sky vapors.
My grandfather's five moons rise
above me. His wife stands clouding
the door of night, blesses me with her once-
fleshy palm, lays it like ivory twigs
upon my head. A holy garment. The chalice
and the cup. She bids me to find blue,
points to the field of night flowers, white

and heavy with damp. I kneel in between
   rows
of petals and stems, scent seeping. Camphor
of night. She bids me to immerse myself in
   water
past the patch of trees. She prays I bear
   children,
that they will swim like truth
around my sphere. She names me
Saturn, and I bow to her presence
in silence, her bones clattering a prayer,
near and around me.

Marian Haddad

Altar para los hombres
TERRY A. YBÁÑEZ
DE SANTIAGO

Nine Ways to Step into a Tree

I.

Three trees sat on three
hills, overlooking the world.
As the first sun rose, their
leaves glistened with knowledge.

II.

My tree is the night,
which must every year
shed her stars.

III.

This ocean/forest has
no end. In every wave,
the world dies, but leaves
its future behind in an acorn
at the water's edge.

IV.

The leaves envelop
me, smooth against
my skin
    feel inside
my bones
    reach down
to my soul.

V.

Nine salmon
sleep within me—
each one full
of fallen worlds.
I feel this through
my skin—my bark
singed by the sparking sky.

VI.

A leaf brushes me as it falls into the
   pool. I
feel its memories across my cheek—
   my chest
heaves—down my calves; spiraling.
   Encased
by wind and rain, I loose my grip, I fall.
    One voice.
The ripple spreads.

VII.

Smoke rises from me in clouds.
I think myself ablaze, yet know
myself to be the flame.

VIII.

I lay beside the pool. With
my fingers, I trace the water
my secrets. Below, they watch
me and know my heart. Still,
I feel the water stir.

IX.

This pot I boil inside myself.
I reach within these mysteries I
find there and recognize worlds
sunk deep and swallowed.

Oisín Mabry

Explosion # 9
RACHEL HECKER

Word Pool for Deep Eddy

My lithe bronze
water snake

strokes through
the lap lane

parting the bug
and leaf litter.

You may send it my way, lovey.
That's what mamas are for.

I admire your
finger catch

your side glide
your endless elegance.

Remember
when I dandled you

between my legs
in the shallow end?

Oh, of course not.
But remember this now:

My pull steadfast
your kick exuberant.

Leslie Morris

to a brown spider: en el cielo
(FOR J. E. C.)

Brave arachnid
spinning with star-lit dreams
your daring web
—how precarious is your perch!
I too h

    a

    n

  g by a thread.

Angela de Hoyos

a una araña sepia: en el cielo
(PARA J. E. C.)

Araña valerosa
que hilas con sueños de estrellas encendidas
tu intrépida tela
—cuán precaria es tu percha!
También yo c

    u

    e

    l

    g

  o de un hilo.

Angela de Hoyos

Bracing Myself to Hear the Day's News

FOR TANJA DRAGIC

This small toy horse
on the shelf
is all I'd take with me
if the leaves of drought were to fall
or if a great voice ordered the river
to rise
and it did.
In these times
a child's eye is our only hope
and hand.
To draw a window
jump through
and erase it from the other side.

Philip Pardi

Pedestal (Hammer)
RACHEL RANTA

For the Elderly Man Whose Heart Gave Out While I Washed Dishes at Twin Sisters Restaurant

i don't want to die hungry
"can i take your order?"
    recently pierced susan asked
no, i'll just have
        cardiac un-rest
    instead
    and then the men in blue
    came and strapped him in
      plastic oxygen
    breathe in breathe out
hope your heart can stand
the pain
this life brings
and i hope to god
i never have to die hungry
allow me to devour
thick-breaded egg salad life

plump vegetarian sandwiches
with soulful avocados
oh so creamy
melt in my heart
and keep it well
so that forty years from now
let me not cry when
She tiptoes in
and asks to
see me outside
let me cry out in joy
when She
sends me to the principal's office
because there is nothing left in
this world
for me to hunger for

Eve Lyons

Names

Lea wants to change her name to Tina.
Her mother says she must think very carefully
    because a name has to fit.
The wrong name can bind like someone else's shoes.
Who knows where a name has walked,
dust of what roads, uncomfortable creases across the toe,
the heel worn down by someone else's sorrow?

Her brother says the name Tina fits.
But if she's Tina, he says, what happened to Lea?
The name turned down the wrong street, got lost,
fell off the edge of the mountain.
The sound of her name fills the river valley.
Everywhere it is nowhere, he says,
her name needs to come home.

Lea doesn't want to be Tina anymore.
It's just too much responsibility.

Michael Simms

Christmas at the Ranch

Uncle hunts in the yellow fields.
In the kitchen, Aunt is baking.
A cup of brown sugar, a stick of butter,
sings the KitchenAid mixer on low.

After breakfast the boys wrestle
with night crawlers and fishing line.
Someone is pricked with a hook,
shouts break out, the fishing ceases.

They shoot BBs at a Coke can
scattering the scrub grass silver.
Aunt is peeling cactus leaves.
Thick tamales crumble to stuffing.

So Mom isn't here, one brother says.
So what. We can eat as much pie
as we want. I might try a beer.
He skips a rock across the pond.

Uncle drives the Jeep back home
with a deer hanging upside down.
The boys watch him pull the steaming
insides out, the slick enormous heart.

Rachel Barenblat

To my country-music-loving daughter, at 12

I'll wait for you
as George Strait might croon
'til we make new country music
'til the li'l dogie in you
decides dad's not so bad.

When you were a babe
I came to your call
like a cow
needing milking,
a ranch hand
to the dinner bell.

Now it's a showdown.
You're the young cowpoke
with something to prove.
I'm the old doc
with bandages,
the grizzled gunslinger,
the sheriff.

You think I'm unnecessary.
Surely I'm not.
Surely we'll realize
the love we hold back.

Darby Riley

Briar Creek Road
MARGIE CRISP

Industrial Landscapes

metal hooks hanging
from a wire on the
band saw, set up out
in the courtyard

                clanking crows

      ✳

the landscape of removal
a sink console unit pulled
from the men's room
now the wall reveals
in peeled-away layers
landscape in browns, rust, grays
     and blacks, a river mud gorge
     bank view
what's left, what's taken

      ✳

the natatorium goes up
     month after tiring month
we're up to the brick facing
       now
and all the hydraulics inside

I'm waiting
amid the haul and hurtle
      for the big hose

Jim LaVilla-Havelin

A stand of flags

They stretch along the creek
bed all the way to the trunk
of the ancient oak. Green swords
pushing toward the Episcopal Church
on the hill. No one remembers who
planted them.

I was never there in spring when
they bloomed but Mama Neil said
the blossoms were as big as a
fist, mauve with yellow centers
and a sweet, sweet smell.

She gave me seven of them
wrapped in old, wet
copies of the *Littleville Gazette,*
used tinfoil and a rubber
band to hold the plastic bag in place.

In Texas they grew almost knee
high—simple fragrant memories of
Mama Neil's little white house
by the side of the road.

I wonder how many springs
will pass in this house before
no one remembers that
their roots were
once covered
in red Alabama dirt?

Cynthia J. Harper

Dream Daddy
KATIE PELL

Radio Silence

He remembers her
once or twice a year,
whenever he sees
olive-skinned women
with hair to the waist.
He shakes his head
and recalls the dark girl
who almost ruined his life.

In her house he sleeps
with the dust mites.
He vibrates in the floorboards
wherever she walks.
She hears him on the radio.
Between stations he hisses
with the death rattle
of distant stars.

Donna Trussell

Dichosa

(There is no hardship that does not bring with it benefit.)

When I think about it now—
Those years when my face betrayed me, wounded me,
No matter how hard I battled,
Leaving me bloodied and scarred,
The mosaic of painful pinks and reds—
I know that I have healed.
Only the tiniest shadows remain
But they don't hurt anymore.

When I think about it now—
Those endless summers
Of detesting the person who stared back at me
From photographs taken at the beach or a birthday party,
The same image that startled me in full-length mirrors at stores
Where the smallest size on the rack was never small enough—
I know that I no longer expect to be the inchoate, innocent child;
I welcome the woman, my body a complete collection of curves.

When I think about it now—
All those years of being the girl
Slumped in the sideline shadows
Waiting for all those boys who never called,
Unwillingly sitting out a million dances
Where everyone else swayed and moved with ease to the same tune—
I know that I don't like the same songs anymore,
I don't have the same moves.

When I got a bad grade,

When the boy didn't like me back,

When I wasn't invited or included,

My mother always attempted to console me saying,

"No hay mal que por bien no venga,"

Wanting me to take heart,

To learn joy from misfortune.

Though part of me remains

Broken and lost in the darkness,

Finally

I shed my skin,

I shattered the "fun-house" mirror,

I found my way out of there,

Moving to the rhythms of grace,

Looking straight ahead.

Yvette Benavides

Earl's

The blue-haired ladies
mash at the crust
of their red cherry pie
with the backs of forks

sip at watery Sanka
all dolled up
with NutraSweet

talk over the gravest faults
of their daughters-in-law
out of the sides
of latticed lips

dab the point of white triangle napkin
to rescue crumbs stuck in pink sunset

push eyeglasses up
into fallen brow's purple cradle

hug stiff purses
to girdled hip by the
crook of a crook of a
dimpled elbow
to powder their powder
after one more cup
after one more cup

Dearie don't you know
they let those Texas vowels hang loose
on topics like
the wayward ways
of other people's grown children
other people's grown children

around four
around four in the afternoon
with the girls
in the dark red cool
of Earl's.

Andréa Greimel

Donuts 2
ELLEN BERMAN

After My Father's Death

I inherit his closet, his polished shoes
shoes with torn insteps and recently replaced soles
I put them on and discover they're a whole size too large
my toes wiggle freely, my heels lift with each step

I walk a block in my father's shoes and keep walking
for, although I now understand why his feet dragged a little
and his aching legs moved cautiously up stairs
I do not understand him

why he was content to be unhappy, why he worked
at what he hated every day of his life
in uniform with his age: itchy woolen sweaters
suit jackets, black socks, starched shirts, trousers

I pack up his things for the Salvation Army
This is the bulk of my father's life
but certainly something must be missing—
I am alarmed at the boxes I carry to my car

imagine men walking around in my father's clothing
hunched under raincoats and worn hats
like me in these oversized shoes and jacket
warm in his bitter fabric

Catherine Kasper

Stars

Her head bowed, the mother is silent now,

weak, with tears on her face; the father's

too weary to push his voice at the boy

any longer, and out of reasons why he should.

The boy, chin pointed at them both,

backs away another step, one hand behind him

reaching for the door he will close on them.

Everything is slowing now, running out, wearing down.

On the table the tepid food lies abandoned.

A cold breath across vast space goes

between them in this silence, and away

from each other they whirl in gigantic arcs.

Reginald Gibbons

The Next Day

So little separates the quick
from the recently dead. It's as if
the glass wall at the far end of Customs
were no longer frosted, and we could see them
clear as yesterday, and they could see us.
Surely they'd want to see us. They
look back. The simplest things have turned
mysterious. They study the marks
on the glass doors. TUO.
TUO? They look at each other.
They shrug and shake their heads.
It must be language, but it's written
in a code they will never, ever,
    decipher.

Sue Wheeler

Leap of Faith #2
SKY PATTERSON

For Brothers Everywhere

There is a schoolyard that runs
from here to the dark's fence
where brothers keep goin to the hoop, keep
risin up with baske'balls ripe as pumpkins
toward rims hung like piñatas, pinned
like thunderclouds to the sky's wide chest
an' everybody is spinnin an' bankin
off the glass, finger-rollin off the glass
with the same soft touch you'd give
the head of a child, *a chile witta*
big-ass pumpkin head, who stands
in the schoolyard lit by brothers—postin up,
givin, goin, taking the lane, flashin off
the pivot, dealin behind the back, between
the legs, cockin the rock an' glidin
like mad hawks—swoopin black with arms
for wings, palmin the sun, throwin it down,
and even with the day gone, without even
a crumb of light from the city, *brothers*
keep runnin-gunnin, fallin away takin

fall-away j's from the corner, their bodies
like muscular saxophones *body-boppin*
better than jazz, beyond summer, beyond
weather, beyond everything that moves—
an' with one shake they're pullin-up
from the perimeter, shakin-bakin,
brothers be sweet pullin-up from
the edge a' the world, hangin like
air itself hangs in the air,
an' gravidy gotta giv'em up: the ball
burning like a fruit with a soul
in their velvet hands, while the wrists
whisper backspin, *an' the fingers comb the*
   rock
once—givin it up, lettin it go, lettin it go
like good news because the hoop is a well,
a well with no bottom, *an' they're*
fillin that sucker up!

Tim Seibles

Georgia O'Keeffe Remembers Texas

When light came to the plains and the evening star rose
I was alone, loving the sky.   Oh, you have never seen such sky!
The evening star was the sound of glass splintering.
I found a door in the square, I painted my way into the world.
No one could teach me what was in my head: the bulging orb,
the undulating line, the flower opening.   Words and I
weren't friends, but every color had its language:
my manic yellow,   red of San Antonio,   my Guadalupe
blossoming green.   I wanted everything all at once, to see
with unprejudiced vision.   I primed blank canvases
and waited for the child of my imagination.   I remember
sleeping in tents, taking the last train to where the windmills
jutted from the plains, the loud saloons, boots
on wooden sidewalks, high nights in Amarillo,
then Palo Duro, first juniper and then the canyon,
a slit in the nothingness, a waterfall, the wind
carrying the lowing of a cow for her calf.   I want nothing now
but to walk into that wide sunset space with the star.
In the end, isn't it all memory?   The flower opening,
the train trailing smoke in the Texas night?

Lee Robinson

Driving at Night to Uvalde

In my old Ford pickup on Highway 90, alongside

The railroad tracks that follow this highway

From Houston to El Paso, driving westward

On a dark night with dark thoughts

And far behind me I hear a freight train coming

Its three headlamps making a luminous tunnel in the darkness

It catches me up, and for a moment

everything is radiant, electrified

The tangled brush and the highway are lit up in black and gold

    A poet's job is to see into things like this

    We wait for a message of hope and courage

    Composed of words we so foolishly threw away

    Waiting for the word from train whistles or

Late-night radio, 1930's cowboy songs,

El Rancherito Del Aire out of Piedras Negras

How often at night

When the heavens are bright

Have I tuned in or tried to tune in

to some comforting music

But the train says *here*! In its long and terrible voice

    Here is the truth and that is you

Are passing through the world like a freight

You have not been here always and someday

You will not be here at all,

It says wake up the West Texas night when it is darkest

It says carry your load straightforwardly in a

Loud and racketing rhythm

Never move without dancing

It says always be sure your engineer is awake and watching the gauges

And the pressures and the joints of the rails

Pouring at you down the long corridor

Of the night hours, do your best

Not to run over the innocent and the foolish

And the drunk and those who have escaped from their

Fences and wandered onto your right-of-way

It says treasure this very moment that I, a

Great and powerful engine,

Am traveling alongside you and lighting your way

Live in it as if it may never happen again

And I am warning you it may not

Remember, in the diesel smoke of my passing

Those who jumped from the burning tower holding hands

Remember my name, the Union Pacific, one

Nation indivisible, and the intricate works of beauty

Spray-painted on my boxcars, my traveling art show

Courtesy of dangerous gifted gang children

In the great cities

That I carry through the desert like flags

Take thought tonight in your decrepit pickup

Of how I show myself only in the absolute darkness

I have come out of nowhere to carry you over the Blanco River bridges

In a storm of light

In your solitude, your dog riding patiently in the back

Remember you hold your own life in your hands

Like a wheel.

Paulette Jiles

River Paradise
MELANIE FAIN

Rune

Under the wind there is a place where you can hide.
Think of it as a silent event. An evening comes,
and you are ready to tell a story you have never
heard, tell it in such a way that whatever secrets
you had gather around you now to listen. They have
no name but yours, and they are still listening.

David Wevill

Untitled
JEONG-JA KIM CODY

NOTES ON THE CONTRIBUTORS

Ann Alejandro's high school English teacher confirms that during her junior year, she skipped school on sixty afternoons to go to the Nueces River. A lifelong resident of Uvalde, she still loves going to the river and fly-fishing for largemouth bass.

Robert A. Ayres spent as much time as possible outdoors when he was a teenager—hunting, fishing, camping, and falling in love with Texas. More or less grown up now, with teenage daughters of his own, he manages his family's ranchland on Barton Creek in the hill country southwest of Austin.

Rachel Barenblat grew up swimming in the Guadalupe River and picking loquats in her front yard. Now that she lives in Massachusetts, the things she misses most about Texas are wildflowers in April, tamales in December, and the big sky year-round.

Wendy Barker: "San Antonio lured me from Berkeley in 1982—I fell in love with this place, with the people, their openness, and with the land. The people now are better than ever, but also more than ever, and the live oaks, the tall grasses, the painted buntings, the roadrunners—they disappear at an alarming rate, and I am not as fed by strip malls and asphalt as I am by the sound of horned owls and whippoorwills at night. So far, we still have the sky."

Yvette Benavides: "I was born and raised on the border in Laredo. My family is proficient in English and Spanish. Sometimes the languages commingle; code switching is a part of my expression at home and in my writing. Spanish is a rich, lyrical, and gorgeous language; the echoes from my childhood that come back to me in memories and reveries are invariably in Spanish."

Ellen Berman attended art school in Austin and Houston. Her work has appeared in galleries and museums all over the state.

Patricia Spears Bigelow: "As a teenager, I listened with envy to my dad and brother's hunting tales. Every fall they dodged wild hogs and rattlesnakes (known as "shorties") while tracking burly South Texas bucks. But after seeing a newly killed whitetail deer, I knew hunting was not for me. Ever since, I've been a stalker of poems instead of wild game."

Robert Bonazzi: "My family traveled by train to Texas from New York City when I was five, to begin a new life. I was excited, expecting to see cowboys and Indians on horseback! It was 103 degrees and we wilted in the humid heat of Houston, which then seemed like a small town. When we returned to New York on vacation, my cousins still believed all Texans carried pistols and herded cattle. After forty years, Texas looks like the rest of America and I haven't ridden a horse yet."

Julie Bozzi lives and paints in Fort Worth.

sharon bridgforth moved to Austin from Los Angeles and is still a touring artist "happy at home in the beauty of Austin fresh air and dreams."

Susan Bright lives in Austin, where she is a year-round lap swimmer at Barton Springs and a board member for Save Barton Creek, an environmental group dedicated to preserving the aquifer in central Texas. She is also publisher for the prolific, feminist *Plain View Press*.

Rolando Briseño lives and paints in San Antonio.

Jenny Browne got her red hair from her great-grandmother Grace, who died the day before Jenny was born. Grace had been living in upstate New York, so they sent her body home to Fort Wayne, Indiana, for burial. It took a while. The railroad workers read "Fort W." and sent her to Fort Worth, Texas, instead. Grace always did want to live in Texas.

Robert Burlingame: "I came to West Texas (I stress the word *west*) to live close to Mexico, its glamour and passionate patience. I taught many students, a great number yet in their teens, at the University of Texas, El Paso. We took, as they say, sweet counsel together. Now I live with my wife, Linda, on a ranch in the Guadalupe Mountains."

Beverly Caldwell: "I was born and raised in Fort Worth. For years I tried to write like the poets I admired. Eventually I relaxed and found my voice and yes—it has a definite Texas twang. I love everything about Texas: its distinctive shape and colorful history, its geographical diversity, its critters, and the wit and wisdom of its people. When I complained to my mother that I couldn't think on my feet the way some people could, she said, 'Well, just sit down.'"

Jacinto Jesús Cardona grew up in Alice, the hub of South Texas, where he often asked the passive parking meters, "Caught in the vortex of oil wells and taco shells, am I Tex or am I Mex, part-time Aztec, or am I your classic borderline case?"

Wendy Taylor Carlisle is an accidental Texan who moved to Texarkana with her husband, a real Texan, and is delighted to find herself still there after fifteen years. She reads to her dog, who has lately shown interest in cowboy poetry.

David Zamora Casas is a painter and performance artist living in a historical cottage in San Antonio.

Rosemary Catacalos: "My family has been in San Antonio since the early 1900s, but both sets of grandparents (who raised me) were immigrants, from Mexico and Greece. So my formative sense of being deeply rooted and profoundly uprooted at the same time has been a major influence on who I am and what I write. Texans are no strangers to paradox!"

John Cates is a painter, elementary school teacher, and passionate soccer fan living in Amarillo.

Sandra Cisneros: "I came to Texas in 1984 because of a job, and because I couldn't wait to run away from home—Chicago. . . . I have made terribly lucky mistakes, like painting my house Mexican colors and not having children of my own, which allows me time to mother other things in my life. I am forever grateful I do not have to get up with an alarm clock or go to work wearing what 'ladies' my age are supposed to wear."

James Cobb is an artist and musician in San Antonio. He plays with the group Pseudo Buddha.

Jeong-Ja Kim Cody grew up in Korea and now lives in Lubbock with her daughter.

Sarah Cortez was born under the beautiful, wide Texan sky in Houston to Mexican and Spanish families whose lives here predated U.S. ownership of Texas. These same endless horizons have seen her as a shy and awkward teenager, a patrol police officer, and a poet. She loves Texas and hopes to live here until she goes feetfirst into another realm.

Margie Crisp lives in Elgin. "When I first moved from the city to our rural home, I became reacquainted with the night. I continue to be fascinated by the mysterious and transformative quality of moonlight."

Valerie Crosswell adopted central Texas as her home in 1977. She loves the deserts, mountains, and endless star-filled sky of West Texas.

Mary Agnes Dalrymple was born in Baytown and grew up in Crosby. When her school integrated with Drew Junior High, she found herself the lone white female face in her class. She says it was the best thing that could have happened to her, a chance to grow away from old attitudes. "Learn all you can about yourself. Be willing to change. And never give up."

Vianna Risa Davila is a young writer from San Antonio currently working as a newspaper reporter.

Angela de Hoyos: "I was born in Old Mexico, but my parents moved our family to San Antonio when I was two. I consider myself more 'Tejana' than 'Mexicana' . . . [but] coming from my bicultural, bilingual upbringing, I cannot say to which 'nation' I owe my sympathy, because I love them both, dearly and equally."

Wendy Dimmette was born on a ranch formed by a bend of the Red River. That rich Texas land is still her place in the sun, and the words of her poetry have a rhythm of the river.

Cyra S. Dumitru moved to Texas a few days after she was married at the age of twenty-two. Now the mother of teenagers, she's met many different kinds of snakes that first alarmed her and "now inspire her admiration."

Daniel Durham of Lubbock likes the barbed-wire distances of Texas. He loves gulf storm seacoasts, landlocked geese, whitetail hills, and the odd volcanic mountains around Fort Davis. "Walt Whitman knew nothing of grass," he says. "Neither do we, we just thrive on it. . . . "

Melanie Fain was born and raised in Texas and lives in the hill country on seven wooded acres. Her paintings emphasize birds, botanicals, and insects. "Nature is my livelihood, my recreation, my comfort, my home."

Robert Fink: "The poem 'Of Age' recalls my high school years in the small East Texas town of Winnsboro, when all my buddy Mark and I had to worry about was surviving football practice and earning enough cash hauling truckloads of drilling mud to oil rigs to be able to fill up the gas tank of my 1955 Ford Fairlane and taunt each other into phoning Janeen or Linda or Sherry or Sylvia and trying not to get turned down for a Saturday night date to the Sulphur Springs Drive-In Theater. We had heard there were lands beyond Dallas. We didn't believe it."

Malou Flato was born and raised in Corpus Christi and now lives and paints alternately in Austin and Pray, Montana.

Fernando Esteban Flores: "Like Texas, my life is a web of endless roads: some smooth, long freeways connecting and interconnecting . . . others ragged, caliche-cut backways. . . . As a child I remember the motion of travel from Laredo to San Antonio to other small and vague South Texas towns. . . . There's a constant transit in my blood, a rocking restlessness. . . . It was on Frio City Road that I first encountered the ice-cream man, El Ice-Creenero, peddling his treats. . . ."

Ken Fontenot: "A short time ago I took my teenage nephew to my favorite spot in Austin—Mount Bonnell. He had never been there before. There was a sunset unmatched by any I'd ever seen. Stephen said, 'Look, Uncle Kenny, it's awesome.' 'I know, my friend,' I said. 'I know.'"

Carrie Fountain grew up in a small town in New Mexico, close to the border with Texas. Texas, for her, has always meant enchantment. In high school, one's prom date was judged almost exclusively by whether she/he was willing to drive all the way to El Paso, where the good restaurants were, for a fancy dinner. She always took her dates to Texas. Now she lives in Austin.

Joseph H. Garcia: "I remember going to Conception Park on holidays and Saturdays. My dad and mom and older relatives would set up the grill and arrange the picnic table while we kids escaped to the creek to explore. We never really found much, but it was fun not finding it, anyway. We were young and invincible."

Reginald Gibbons: "I grew up in a semirural area that seemed very far from downtown Houston and is now well within the city limits. Where there were only open fields beyond our houses, there are now countless apartments. . . . The two-lane blacktop that wound through those fields is now a four-lane city street, and our two acres are now paved over. So our feelings, too, are always being built over by new experiences, as one sensation replaces another, one period of our lives gives way to another. Yet someone's poem can refresh our sense of our own gone emotional places and restore us to a deeper sense of ourselves and what we share, in this life, with others."

Rodney Gomez grew up in Brownsville and attended Yale University. "I spent my teenage years in that strip of borderland called Brownsville, Texas. I didn't travel beyond that small space until I was eighteen, and I never knew anything different. Even Mexico was a foreign place to me. But who needed anything else in an area so drenched with history and good people and life stories? My memory of home is so strong and touches so much of everything I do—from learning the law to writing poetry—that I intend to return to the Valley and make my home there."

Ray Gonzalez grew up in El Paso. He has since taught and edited journals and anthologies in many American cities.

Larry Graeber began exhibiting his paintings, drawings, and sculpture twenty-seven years ago. He lives in San Antonio.

Lyman Grant was founder of *Man!* magazine and has resided, edited, and taught in central Texas for a long time. "I have lived several lives so far. . . ."

Andréa Greimel: "Born and raised in Minnesota, I grew up among farmer-labor Democrats for whom Texas was a land where ruthless capitalists reigned with no social/humanitarian/environmental strings attached. 'How can you live in a state without an income tax?' they asked. I came to Texas from Mexico, where I worked after college. Here in San Antonio I have found that the politics of my upbringing resonate very well, especially in the magnificent Chicano community in which I teach."

Marian Haddad was born in El Paso to an older Syrian immigrant couple who already had eight children born in Juwaikat, near Damascus. "I am American. I am Syrian. I am, at my core, Texan." After living around the United States, she returned to "the rich cultural traditions of Texas, the *conjunto* music and corridas, Texas blues, two-stepping country, folk, and Americana songs." She loves fiery sunsets atop the desert Franklin Mountains, hard rains of south central Texas, and the big Texas sky.

Isabeth Bakke Hardy is a painter originally from San Antonio who founded the legendary New Age School (now called Circle School) for young children.

Cynthia J. Harper: "My garden in San Antonio blooms for twelve months every year—roses, bougainvillea, asters, mums, snapdragons, hibiscus, and little Johnny-jump-ups. In Ohio, where I grew up, I helped my mom plant marigolds and tomatoes, but they were gone in September. Texas never stops blooming."

Carla Hartsfield: "I was born in Waxahachie. My mother's family name, Milam, goes all the way back to Colonel Ben Milam, one of thirty-six brave men who defended and lost their lives at the Alamo. So my roots in Texas go very deep. When I moved to Canada in 1982, I took a book of Texas wildflowers with me. Every spring when it's still snowing in Toronto I get out my wildflower book and imagine myself walking through those vast Texas fields."

Billy Hassell was born in Dallas and now lives in Fort Worth. He has shown his paintings and been a visiting artist all over the United States.

Sheila S. Hatch was born and raised in San Antonio, where she grew to love pink and violet sunsets, late-night conversations on the back patio, and Tex-Mex food.

Rachel Hecker lives and works in Houston. A recent show of her work was called *Sad and Pissed: New Paintings*.

Fran Hillyer of Dallas is a native Texan, born from native Texan parents, whose parents were native Texans. Her great-great-grandfather signed the Declaration of Independence for the Republic of Texas. As a teenager in Austin, she wanted to see the world, but the live oaks she climbed as a child seemed to recall her to their arms.

Edward Hirsch lived in Houston for eighteen years. In 2003, he took off his hat and moved to New York City, where he is now the president of the John Simon Guggenheim Memorial Foundation.

James Hoggard was born in Wichita Falls, where he now lives. As a boy he spent a lot of time in woods and rivers near his home. He ran a trapline and went outside in the middle of the night to study the ways in which the constellations had shifted since bedtime. In his senior year of high school, as he was rigorously developing his poetic craft, he was a three-year letterman on the state championship football team.

John Igo: "I grew up on the edge of the hill country just northwest of San Antonio, a location chosen by my German ancestors because it reminded them of their homeland. Until I was an adult, it was resonantly natural, with urban sprawl decades away. It has nurtured all my writing."

Paulette Jiles resides in a San Antonio neighborhood of historic old houses and artists with purple hair and the spirits of cattlemen and clockmakers and the occasional hailstorm.

Roger Jones teaches in the beautiful town of San Marcos.

Ben Judson: "Certainly the character of Texas is more complex than many want to believe: there *are* trees here; some of my oldest friends are trees. When I am acutely aware of my disconnection from the world, it is those branches that have always reached into my mind and dissolved the space between my feet and the soil."

Catherine Kasper can no longer live without fresh salsa and homemade tortillas, or breakfast *migas* (which uses both of those), which her "Texas-grown" husband first prepared for her ten years ago in Chicago.

Daniel Kelly is a young painter in San Antonio.

Deborah Maverick Kelley is a member of the legendary Maverick family. She has lived in Michigan, Rhode Island, and Texas.

Ronald Kolodzie was a fashion designer in New York City for many years and currently paints and runs a studio in San Antonio, his hometown.

Jim LaVilla-Havelin moved to Texas to be the first director of the San Antonio Children's Museum. The view of the Window at Chisos Basin in Big Bend, the color of a vermilion flycatcher, Christmas tamales, and oceans of bluebonnets got into his blood. "Not Jimbob, and not the Havelin of javelinas. . . . In junior high, because some nicknames are meant for irony and inappropriateness, for a time I was called Tex."

Annette Lawrence lives and teaches in Denton and works as a visual artist in a range of two- and three-dimensional mediums.

Pedro Luján grew up in El Paso. His paintings have been described as "emotionally charged energy fields of haunting psychic imagery. Primary forms like the circle, the spiral, and the zigzag are activated through luminous coloration and expressive gestural brushwork." (Tomas Ybarra-Frausto)

Eve Lyons views being Texan as an aspect of her identity like ethnicity—something that is part of her, for better and for worse. She has been described by others as a "Jewish bisexual vegetarian writer." Despite her current residence out of state, she remains an avid and obsessed Spurs fan and Mexican food snob.

Oisín Mabry, a native of San Antonio, was first inspired while dangling from a pier in Corpus Christi. Since then, he has been amazed by the stars of West Texas, followed the Marfa Lights, gotten lost in the trees of the hill country, and almost been eaten by an alligator on the Louisiana border.

Ignacio R. Magaloni: "I love teaching English and creative writing classes at Northwest Vista College in San Antonio. . . . Texans are expert friend makers, and with so many Texans smiling at each other in my classes—well, I only wish you could join us!"

Marissa C. Martínez comes from a long ancestral history in Texas, her ancestors having arrived in 1760. She appreciates family gatherings in Texas—tortillas warming on the griddle, big *platos de carne* or tamales, two languages interwoven, cousins and more cousins, everyone sharing stories—which have changed little despite the farther-flung nature of the family.

Khaled Mattawa was born in Libya and now lives, teaches, and translates contemporary Arabic poetry into English in Austin.

Marcy McChesney is a young painter living in San Antonio.

Walt McDonald lives in Lubbock with "the strangeness of flat Texas plains—the hauntingly wide horizons, the splendor of it all" where he grew up. He moved to Colorado as a newlywed but came back to Texas. "For years I had not considered this world to be my home. But when I let down my bucket in the Texas plains, I found all sorts of metaphors and images for poems. . . . "

Julia McLernon, better known as Rabbitt, was "never the dainty, demure girl her mother wanted." She favors cats, horses, and purple, while finding "little use for panty hose, conservatives, and artists' bios."

Christopher Middleton: "Born in Cornwall, England. After thirty-five years in and around Austin (though I travel far afield), I am still an expatriate from Europe, rather than a Texan. If I've taken on any color from this milieu, it would not be that of the boastful species, but of the rustic. Nor do I forget that Texas is the Siberia of Mexico."

Alberto Mijangos grew up in Mexico and lives and paints in San Antonio. He has said, "We have to have the guts to search for the eternal in the dark. This is the only way we can be deeply moved." A recent show of his works was called *Trusting the Darkness.*

Bryce Milligan grew up in Dallas, climbing trees and exploring creeks. He once floated down the Trinity River on a homemade raft, emulating his hero, Huckleberry Finn. By sixth grade he had read that book so many times that his mother hid it from him. Christmases and summers were spent in White Deer, a small town on the high plains of Texas. He drove a tractor on his grandfather's farm and composed songs in his head during solitary hours. He wrote them down on the small pad always in his pocket. To this day, his best ideas come while driving, alone with the windows open and headed west.

Michael A. Moore moved to Texas when he married. He joined the Japan-America Society and began writing haiku poetry, which he would later teach to students in the San Antonio Botanical Gardens. Now he lives south of Dallas.

Trey Moore: "I am a carpenter poet, born in San Anto. I am the land. Favorite place in Texas: Guadalupe Mountains National Park. I lived here all my life."

Pat Mora: "I was born and spent most of my life in El Paso. My grandparents had all crossed the Rio Grande and settled in El Paso at the time of the Mexican revolution. Since none of my grandparents spoke English, my parents were the translating generation in their homes. I've always lived in two languages, in two worlds."

Leslie Morris moved to Texas after living in Indonesia and Burma. She thinks Texas is one of the most exotic places she has ever lived and that Austin's Deep Eddy Pool is one of the world's loveliest lap pools.

Moira Muldoon: "I grew up in Texas and couldn't wait to leave. I wasn't more than a semester or two into college, however, before I realized how unusual the place was I'd left behind: None of my roommates had learned the Cotton Eyed Joe in fifth grade PE class or had an entire year of state history in junior high. Texas was bolder, prouder, warmer, silly square-dancin'er than Oregon or Massachusetts or Ohio. And that's a big part of why I moved back."

Harryette Mullen lived all over Texas—Galveston, Beaumont, and Mount Pleasant, among other places—for half her life. "What I miss about Texas: family, friends, Tex-Mex food, barbeque the way I like it, starry skies, bluebonnets. What I don't miss: the smell of oil refineries, triple-digit summers, cockroaches, cowboy stuff, chicken-fried steak, tornadoes."

Jack Myers: "When I got out of grad school, there were few jobs for poets. For three years, in blistering Boston summers and freezing winters, I painted houses, department stores, water towers, Harvard University (I remember looking through the window I was painting and thinking I should be inside teaching, not outside painting) in order to support my family. Finally I got a job teaching poetry writing in Texas. So when they say, 'Texas is a state of mind,' it's been heaven for me. Now I feel I am inside looking out and I am eternally grateful for that." He is currently poet laureate of Texas.

Dave Oliphant was born in Fort Worth but grew up in Beaumont. "The South Park district where we lived was home to oil refinery workers, and our neighbors included many Italian and French Cajun families. . . .While most students were listening to Elvis Presley, I was introduced to jazz by my orchestra teacher. . . . Neither jazz nor poetry has for me ever gone out of style."

Barbara Orlovsky: "No one 'back home' in Massachusetts understands my twenty-eight happy years of exile in Texas—real football and ranching and the long, long highways we camped along when my children were young. My father said the landscape was like Mars—to me it is blessed by talking sky, strange insects, and sere plants. Lots of room for old and young teens to roam."

Radames Ortiz: "The vast openness of the American Southwest has always affected me. Though I have always lived in Houston, I still feel a close connection to the rural desert landscape of my parents' land and home. The Southwest has become the very fabric of my life and poetry."

Paula Owen is the director of the Southwest School of Art and Craft. "Isolation has been a recurring subtext in my work and it was heightened by moving to South Texas, but the move also brought me back in touch with the landscape and the natural world, which are my real passions."

Yu Cha Pak grew up in Korea and lives in Houston. She has illustrated children's books, including Naomi Shihab Nye's *Benito's Dream Bottle*.

Aaron Parazette lives and paints in Houston. He shows his work through Texas Gallery.

Philip Pardi moved to Austin in 2000 to attend the Michener Center for Writers. He loves the ever-available breakfast tacos, the countless grackles, and the bumper stickers that read: "I wasn't born in Texas, but I got here as fast as I could!"

Scottie Parsons lives and paints in north Texas.

Sky Patterson is the grandson of Hondo Crouch, the colorful Texas folk hero who owned the legendary town of Luckenbach. He has been active in many artistic genres since the age of seven and currently lives and paints on his family's ranch near Comfort. "Having experienced being a teenager as well as being an artist, I noticed two things in common. Both are considered somewhat outsiders and both are driven by a smoldering angst."

Katie Pell currently operates a painting and ceramic studio in what used to be a grocery store in old downtown San Antonio. (The front window still says SHRIMP.) Her dogs are named Punko and Squeeze. She is attracted to the use of narrative in her paintings. "I think it's true that history is made up of seconds and I plan to document many of the insignificant (and imaginary) ones."

Andrea Peyton lives on a ranch with horses, chickens, and her husband, Jim Peyton, who writes Mexican food cookbooks. Her paintings of wildlife have been widely exhibited. She is a member of Bat Conservation International and has traveled extensively in Africa.

Robert Phillips directs the Creative Writing Program at the University of Houston. His greatest Texas-related worry is fear of being served another piece of apple pie laced with jalapeño peppers.

Moumin Manzoor Quazi: "I was born in California, son of an immigrant father from India/Pakistan and an American mother. When I was five, we moved to north central Texas where I grew up, when I wasn't visiting my father in Europe, where he was stationed. Now I live in San Antonio and teach English at the University of the Incarnate Word. With this background, I feel an intimate connection with the migrant birds in my poem."

Rainey lives, paints, and teaches in San Antonio. She has worked with middle school students in the Artists in the Making Program.

Rachel Ranta was born in Minnesota but has lived and painted in Houston for many years.

Darby Riley: "I was born in San Antonio in 1950. In seventh and eighth grades I had a neighborhood paper route. We paperboys roamed over several urban square miles on bicycles at all hours of the day and night—joyful liberty for a kid!"

Geoff Rips: "I grew up in San Antonio and now live in Austin. South Texas once seemed like it was far away from the rest of the world. The world is much smaller now and I'm much older. But you can still find those places, like a wetland lagoon, where the rest of the world seems like a distant memory."

Lee Robinson practiced law in South Carolina for over twenty years but now makes her home in the Texas hill country, on a small ranch near Comfort. She loves exploring the back roads of Texas with her husband.

Omar Rodriguez lives and paints in San Antonio. He is married to Veronica Prida, the legendary designer.

Margie McCreless Roe was born in Fort Worth and has lived somewhere in Texas all her life. She enjoys Mexican food, Fiesta in San Antonio, and memories of grandparents, uncles, and aunts.

Del Marie Rogers: "I was a teenager in Dallas when it was a calmer place. Towns near Dallas have been important for my poetry, including East Plano and Rowlett, near lakes. I love the Davis Mountains of deep southwest Texas, where my mother lived for years."

Reginald Rowe was born in Brooklyn but has lived, painted daily, and taught in San Antonio for many years. "For the last twenty years, my paintings have been mostly shaped canvases where the form of the canvas itself is the dominant imagery of the piece. . . . For many artists art is a vehicle for their concerns with society's problems. For me, art is to be looked at—and with the same intensity and concern as when listening to Mozart or Duke Ellington."

Benjamin Alire Sáenz lives, teaches, writes, and paints in El Paso.

Richard Sale: "I grew up in the Texas oil fields and attended a tiny South Texas high school in Odem—graduating class numbering sixteen. I lucked into lovely English teachers at Del Mar College (Corpus Christi), who saved me from joining the Foreign Legion. A year of teaching in North Africa taught me that I loved my home state with passion. I keep planning to write Poems of Universal Truth, but continue to write Texas ones."

John Phillip Santos: "Texas made it impossible to be anything but a teenager in deep time. Petroglyphs, mission ruins, downtown San Antonio, the Nueces River—beacons of ancient Texas earth." His first book, about growing up in Texas, was a National Book Award finalist.

F. J. Schaack has been teaching in Texas for many years—in Boerne, San Antonio, Garland, Arlington, Round Rock, and currently Austin. What's kept him, his wife, and six kids in Texas is the expanse—of ethnic diversity, landscape, opportunities, and the people's spirit of *tejas* (friendship).

Tim Seibles: "I came to Texas in 1973, eighteen years old, beginning college at Southern Methodist University in Dallas. It was the place where I discovered tacos. As far as I knew, there were no such things in Philadelphia, city of my birth."

Naomi Stroud Simmons: "Born in Amarillo just before the Depression. Thought all addresses ended in Texas until a trip to California. Imagined I could do anything if given the opportunity—like dance with Fred Astaire . . . write like Ogden Nash. Now I live in Fort Worth and still think all things are possible."

Michael Simms grew up in Houston. He now lives in Pennsylvania and misses his home state terribly. He hasn't had a decent tamale since he left.

Carol M. Siskovic came to Texas to teach teenagers, but for over thirty years they have taught and inspired her. "Like unexpected blue northers or whipping desert whirlwinds, like peaceful Texas lakes or deep, colorful canyons, like flash floods and fandangos, like rodeos and roundups . . . teenagers spark poetry in my life."

Travis Ian Smith: "Central Texas erupts with floral life in springtime and summertime. Daffodils, purple-bearded irises, tulips, Indian paintbrush, Mexican hats, wild thistleflowers, and of course, bluebonnets . . . but my favorite is the red hibiscus, which reigns in July and August. Sometimes the blooms are as large as one's face."

Bruce Snider lives in Austin, where he appreciates the joys of Texas barbecue, fried okra, and chicken enchiladas.

Julie Speed lives and paints in Austin. A series of recent paintings was called *Altars of My Ancestors*. "Sometimes, I swear I can hear them talking amongst themselves, especially if it's late at night."

Gael Stack lives and paints in Houston. She was named 1997 Texas Artist of the Year by the Art League of Houston.

Carmen Tafolla is a prolific poet and stage presence in South Texas.

Sandra Gail Teichmann is pleased to have spent the last eight years in the Texas Panhandle, where her father was born in 1915. Perhaps she has come to understand him more clearly having had for herself "the experience of wide-open Texas skies, playa lakes violet in the morning sun, and the lace of mesquite rooted to an alluvial plain, flat to the horizon and mostly void of motor traffic. It has been good in this overpopulated world at the new millennium to be able to focus on the simplicity of telephone lines—three on the cross beam, one on the apex—reaching for infinity into a distance of windmills twirling as if they . . . indeed do believe in the heavens and the Ogallala Aquifer."

Thom the World Poet loves open mikes in Austin, Texas. He runs regular poetry programs at the Baha'i Center, the Kung Fu Athletic Academy, and the Ruta Maya coffeehouse.

Bruce Tindall of Dallas moved to Texas on the first day of the summerlong drought of 1999. A few weeks later, the dry, cracked soil and fallen trees inspired his poem included in this book.

Jan Tips lives and paints in San Antonio and travels regularly to a country place near Blanco, where her dogs love to run in the fields. Her work has been widely exhibited.

Robert Trammell: "I am working on a book set in East Texas's Gregg County, an essential Texas county. It is home of the red, white, and blue Kilgore Rangerettes, wild honky-tonks, great blues and country music, and Van Cliburn, who in the middle of the Cold War in the 1950s conquered Russia with his piano. Over thirty thousand oil wells have been dug there, and deep in those piney woods are small shacks where some of the best barbecue in the state can be eaten. Few places have better stories."

Ben Tremillo: "San Antonio is a city that whispers. It doesn't really shout. As teens, my friends and I went to all the local haunts, we sought out the ghosts and legends, we cruised Military Drive, we talked, we laughed. All along, the south side was quietly telling me its story. Only now do I really listen."

Donna Trussell is a fifth-generation Texan who grew up in Dallas. When she was sixteen, she worked at her all-time favorite job: tour guide at the Sam Houston Memorial Museum. Today she works among polite and always appropriate midwesterners and deeply misses her home state.

Patty Turner was born, raised, and still lives in Dallas. Because her roots go deep, someday she will be buried there too, next to her parents, grandparents, and great-grandparents. She spent numerous summer childhood vacations on Galveston Island, as do many native Texans.

Leslie Ullman: "My part of Texas is Chihuahuan desert, border country. I have come to feel at home with the spice and dryness and light and stark beauty here, as well as the mix of cultures. I ride my horse through the sand hills and feel myself knitted a little deeper, every time, into this land."

Vincent Valdez is a young painter from San Antonio, recently named Artist of the Year by the Art League.

David Ray Vance: "I was seventeen when I became a vegetarian, which in Fort Worth, Texas, was just shy of proclaiming oneself a traitor to all that is Texan. Later I moved to Austin and discovered that there were Texan vegetarians galore, and that we had our own restaurants. Not just that, but I learned that in addition to the Republican Party, there was also this party called the Democrats, and a couple others to boot. Texans are always talking about how big the state is, but what we really mean to say is that it takes all kinds—and it does."

Bettie Ward: "During my childhood, I galloped over rattlesnakes, being careful not to let my horse get bit. My rancher daddy struck oil, raced Thoroughbreds, and covered my mother and me in diamonds. I was seated next to John Wayne at the rodeo while he was making *The Alamo*. . . . My art is about growth, change, romance, fragmentation, transformation, natural phenomenon, the earth as home, cycles, relationships, and nature as it relates to man. The works teach me about the fragility of life and the benevolence and generosity of mankind."

Mobi Warren moved to Texas when she was six. "On our long, hot drive we encountered an awesome migration of tarantulas that brought all human traffic to a halt. Thus was initiated my lifelong respect and relationship to the animal keepers of Texas. As a storyteller, teacher, and wildlife rescue volunteer . . . I draw my most intimate insights from the animal world."

Phil West moved to Austin from Seattle. "At first I wondered why everything looked so deserted at three in the afternoon. It only took me a few walks to realize what you're supposed to do at three when it's a hundred degrees, and walking's not on that list. I now say 'y'all' and mean it, I like country music (but only if it's real country), and though something about 'breakfast tacos' seemed incongruous and wrong, they've led me to adopt the philosophy of 'How can it be wrong if it feels so right?'"

David Wevill, a Canadian born in Japan, has been teaching poetry to countless lucky students through the University of Texas in Austin for many years.

Sue Wheeler: "I grew up in Austin and went to summer camp in the hill country near Kerrville. The images of Texas I carry with me are those old, round cedary hills, the pale stone, bluebonnets, and the rivers where we swam—the Colorado and the Guadalupe, beautiful names for beautiful waters."

Edward E. Wilson grew up in the Panhandle of Texas in a small town of 374 people that has been the title of a film and location of an ice cream commercial. This place and the characters there occupy much of his writing. "Because there were so few of us, our differences stood out in bold relief against the stark Texas sky."

Steve Wilson: "Although I've traveled all over the world, since I was eleven I have called Texas home. At twelve I went to Scout Camp near San Marcos, at El Rancho Cima, and slept on top of a hill that was bare but for one scraggly mesquite tree. Whenever I drive along Rural Route 32 now, past the camp, I can still see the hill, and that same tree."

Christian Wiman: "I spent the first eighteen years of my life in rural West Texas. When I was in high school, nothing seemed duller or deader to me than the tiny town where my family lived. Now, after living in dozens of cities and several foreign countries, and after finding myself repeatedly writing about that town, few places feel more alive. I just wish I'd paid closer attention."

Terry A. Ybáñez de Santiago lives, paints, and teaches middle school art in San Antonio, after a recent stint teaching in Kuwait. She has painted luminous murals on the sides of inner city buildings.

ACKNOWLEDGMENTS

Naomi Shihab Nye is grateful to the Davis Gallery in Austin, the Texas Gallery in Houston, and Salon Mijangos in San Antonio for their help in locating artists. Also, thanks to Martha Mihalick for her invaluable assistance and Paul Zakris and Virginia Duncan for their brilliance and belief!

With a toast to Dorothy Stafford, favorite honorary Texan, and Charles Butt, favorite native Texan—VIVA!

With gratitude to the Lannan Foundation.

The scope of this volume made it occasionally difficult—despite sincere and sustained effort—to locate poets and artists and/or their executors. The compiler and editor regret any omissions or errors, and will make any necessary corrections in subsequent printings. Permission to reprint copyrighted material is gratefully acknowledged to the following:

ANN ALEJANDRO, for "I Know a Thinger Two," copyright © 2004 by Ann Alejandro. Printed by permission of the author.

ROBERT A. AYRES, for "The Orchard," copyright © 1996 by Robert A. Ayres, first appeared in *The Marlboro Review,* No. 2, (Summer/Fall, 1996). Reprinted by permission of the author.

RACHEL BARENBLAT, for "Christmas at the Ranch," copyright © 2002 by Rachel Barenblat, first appeared in *The Texas Observer,* January 18, 2002. Reprinted by permission of the author.

WENDY BARKER, for "Near Gale," "Cirrocumulus Undulatus," "Cirrus Fibratus," "Altocumulus, Mackerel Sky," copyright © 2004 by Wendy Barker. Printed by permission of the author.

YVETTE BENAVIDES, for "Dichosa," copyright © 2004 by Yvette Benavides. Printed by permission of the author.

ELLEN BERMAN, for *Donuts 2,* copyright © 2000 by Ellen Berman. Reproduced by permission of the artist.

PATRICIA SPEARS BIGELOW, for "Deer Kiln," copyright © 1996 by Patricia Lynn Spears, published by Pecan Grove Press of St. Mary's University, San Antonio, Texas. Reprinted by permission of the author.

ROBERT BONAZZI, for "Ah Words," copyright © 1979 by Robert Bonazzi, from *Fictive Music: Prose Poems* by Robert Bonazzi, published by Wings Press, Houston, Texas. Reprinted by permission of the author.

JULIE BOZZI, for *Dead Grasses,* copyright © 1997 by Julie Bozzi. Reproduced courtesy of Texas Gallery.

SHARON BRIDGFORTH, for an excerpt from "con flama," copyright © 2002 by sharon bridgforth. Printed by permission of the author.

SUSAN BRIGHT, for "Strike Zone," copyright © 1997 by Susan Bright, from *Wind Eyes: A Women's Reader and Writing Source* edited by Susan Bright and Margo LaGalluta, published by Plain View Press. Reprinted by permission of the author.

ROLANDO BRISEÑO, for *San Antonio Fatso Watso Table,* copyright © 1995 by Rolando Briseño. Reproduced by permission of the artist.

JENNY BROWNE, for "Now, That Is Summer," copyright © 2004 by Jenny Browne. Printed by permission of the author.

ROBERT BURLINGAME, for "Connecting," copyright © 1999 by Robert Burlingame, first appeared in *The Rio Grande Review,* Spring/Summer, 1999. Reprinted by permission of the author.

BEVERLY CALDWELL, for "And Every Town Its Dairy Queen," copyright © 2001 by Beverly Caldwell, from *Life Sentences,* a poetry chapbook published by Trilobite Press, Denton, Texas. Reprinted by permission of the author.

JACINTO JESÚS CARDONA, for "Avocado Avenue," copyright © 1998 by Jacinto J. Cardona, published by Chili Verde Press, San Antonio, Texas. Printed by permission of the author.

WENDY TAYLOR CARLISLE, for "Thirteen," copyright © 2004 by Wendy Taylor Carlisle. Printed by permission of the author.

DAVID ZAMORA CASAS, for *Santo Niño Perdido, Rey de Los Angeles de Portiuncula,* copyright © by David Zamora Casas.

ROSEMARY CATACALOS, for "David Talamántez on the Last Day of Second Grade," copyright © 1995 by Rosemary Catacalos, first appeared in *The Texas Observer,* reprinted in *Best American Poetry,* published by Charles Scribner's Sons, 1996. Reprinted by permission of the author.

INDEX TO POEMS

INDEX TO ARTISTS AND POETS

LIST OF ILLUSTRATIONS

xas Being a Couch Potato Can Take Some Work

al Angora Goat Sale Successful

sance Bats in the Big Bend

uture, Heart in Past

tten History, But a Cemetery's Stones Remain

itors Cowboys Rodeo in August

Balloon to Visit Marathon for Big Bend Bash

ews on Speed Bump

ini Cheer Camp Next Week

ation Living High-Wire Life

chy Flea Problem Causes Courthouse Closure

o Save 12 Chisos Lodge Rooms

Don't Mess with Te

DATE DUE

THE LIBRARY STORE #47-0204